Heal Yourself with Color

Walaa

To You,
May you remember the power within you to break
through your conditioning so you can be seen.

Published by Welbeck Balance
An imprint of Welbeck Publishing Group
20 Mortimer Street
London W1T 3JW

First published by Welbeck Balance in 2021
Text copyright © Walaa AlMuhaiteeb, 2021

Walaa AlMuhaiteeb has asserted her right under the Copyright,
Designs and Patents Act, 1988, to be identified as the Author of this work.

A CIP catalogue record for this book is available from the British Library

Printed in Dubai

ISBNS
UK – 978-1-859-06474-0
US – 978-1-800-69062-2

Design by Stacey Jessop

10 9 8 7 6 5 4 3 2

Note/Disclaimer

www.welbeckpublishing.com

Heal Yourself with Color

HARNESS THE POWER OF COLOR
TO CHANGE YOUR LIFE

Walaa

WELBECK
BALANCE

Contents

Hi I'm
Walaa!

I'm a colour therapist and colour specialist – but just consider me your super-wise mentor and bestie who wants to help you get back in balance, find confidence and stop living on auto-pilot.

Does it seem like you can't pick yourself up no matter what you do? You want to learn how to love and appreciate yourself, be able to deal with demanding situations and find joy and happiness again, but right now, you're finding that challenging. Your energy has depleted, you can't seem to overcome the difficult situations that you're faced with and happiness has dangerously drained you.

I work with women who want to distance themselves from toxic relationships and the baggage they come with, open their heart to new love, feel refuelled, refreshed and calm, and appreciate themselves and everything that life has to offer.

As we work together throughout this book, I'll encourage you to spiritually and emotionally evolve, give you as much support as you need to move beyond fear, and help you get out of those toxic relationships and live a magical life. By the time our work is done you'll find a calm inside yourself that you never knew existed; you'll learn the importance of self-love and have a fuller appreciation for life.

Walaa xx

Introduction

*'Colour is a power which directly
influences the soul.'*

Wassily Kandinsky

This book is filled with colours, each included with a certain intention. The colours are here to awaken your intuition. They are here to challenge you and get you out of your comfort zone, where you will find your true inner voice and true self, like I did.

Colours are never straightforward: when you analyze someone's body language, for instance, you need to observe them carefully before being able to understand the full story. You can't look at them biting their nails and say they are nervous – it could simply be a habit, so you have to look at the entire body. When working with colour, you need to step away from the mind in order to feel and experience colour in connection with your body and your feelings. I want you to notice the shift as you move from a place of 'I think' to 'I feel'.

When you do the exercises in this book, uncomfortable feelings might emerge, and when they do, acknowledge them by naming them, embracing them and then releasing them. Allow yourself to fully experience this book with your body and emotions, and your soul will reveal itself to you.

The basics of colour, the story of each colour, the messages they communicate and exercises to help you connect deeply with your inner self are all explained on the following pages. I'll also share some colour hacks I've learned along the way. By the end, you'll develop the skills in order to feel colour on your own and to understand your experiences through them.

My Story: How Colour Changed My Life

Colour is one of the most powerful tools that we have to understand energy, emotions, ourselves and the world. To see a colour, light receptors in our eye transmit the reflected light off an object into our visual cortex where we perceive the colour; at the same time, some retinal cells also send signals to the hypothalamus, which is able to control body temperature, metabolism, sleeping, behavioural patterns and appetite. So colour is so much more than what we see. Colour is a perception. It's our brain's translation of light vibrations, and it might not be exactly how the object looks in the world but how we experience it. The first time I heard that, I had an epiphany, and suddenly it all made sense. This is why our colour choices reflect our subconscious. We see colour in our dreams and colour is part of our aura – the energy fields around us that are generated by our thoughts, emotions and physical body – and thanks to Kirlian photography we can now see what our aura colours look like. Colour is around us daily, affecting us in a positive or negative way, even physically; for instance, too much exposure to blue light from our screens can sometimes lead to retina damage.

Colour provides a powerful map to navigate through our inner world, which, when unguided, can often feel complicated and confusing. Colour stirs our emotions in ways that most of the time we don't understand. It helps us to heal; it provides us with information about what we need, reveals our hidden talents and what our souls are yearning for and it brings joy into our lives. It also takes us into our darkest places to show us what we need more of, what needs to be shifted and what needs to change.

Colour is our map to a world that we don't fully understand – our inner world, our unconscious mind and our emotions. Colour helps us to understand our emotions, what we are searching for, what we need. Whenever we are attracted to a colour, it's a message from our subconscious mind that we need to heal, take action or change something in our lives. Colour helps us find what we are seeking by speaking directly to our subconscious mind.

Take a moment and imagine the room around you without colour. Would it feel the same? Exactly, it wouldn't. It wouldn't bring out in you the same emotions, complexity or depth of expression.

The universe has given us everything we need to grow and to connect with the grace within us. We can lose our way or get confused, but colour is always there to guide us. I see colour as our gift from the sun. It's the magical map that is in front of all of us; it's so simple that we overlook it.

This book gives the gift of colour to you and me. I'm just a vessel that has been transformed by colour and, since then, all I have wanted to do is to share this knowledge. Colour has given me transformation, healing and love beyond measure. Colour gave me life. It introduced me to my true self.

My story starts with my origins. I come from Kuwait, a small country in the Middle East. Every colour has shadow and light aspects to it, and I was born into a world that was filled with the shadow side of colour – the challenging parts that can bring struggle.

I lived a life that was filled with fear. My life took me through a journey of pain, neglect and abuse. I was addicted to pain in all its forms: stress, anxiety, problems and drama, you name it. I identified with pain and I didn't know what the other side of things looked like, until one night when I was feeling that my life had no meaning or purpose, everything changed. I want to tell you about my story because I want you to know that, no matter how black things look around you, the blackness holds a vast well of knowledge within it.

I grew up in a conservative culture, which has very specific ideas about how women should behave. As a woman, I wasn't allowed much freedom and I needed a guardian, which needed to be a male figure in my family, either my father, brother or later my husband, to decide everything for me, from whom I loved, to what I studied, who I could be friends with or when I could travel on my own. I also had a mother who had an even more specific idea of who I must become; this way of living destroyed my

curious, feminine soul. I reached the age of twenty-two believing that I was unable to decide anything for myself, thinking I knew nothing, feeling that my existence was a mistake because I was different from others in my culture and I wanted things that weren't acceptable to those around me. My low confidence hid underneath a 'mean girl' act, and I externalized my pain on to others. I went from one problem to another, not knowing the difference between happiness and misery.

From an early age I had ideas that strongly clashed with the culture I was born into; I believed I had the right to make mistakes and that I shouldn't have to believe everything I was told. I used to cry to the moon when I had difficulties. I knew there were some healing powers there and people around me told me I was crazy. I questioned cultural norms, and I felt that those ideals didn't represent me. I was born into a culture that didn't want me to think differently or make the bold choices I wanted to make.

Both my parents struggled with my strong need to rebel: my father escaped it, my mother did her best to contain it, and I didn't want to be contained. I got married as an escape from this reality, believing it was true love. But I didn't know or love myself, so the universe handed me back my inner world, with my escape turning into just another form of chaos, reflecting the chaos I had within.

One day, during my time at university, I met the man that would become my husband. He was a free thinker, like I was, and we fell in love. He amazed me, as he represented everything I wanted – he was determined, strong and loved me like nobody had before. Thinking back, I see why it became as toxic as it did from the start but I loved him and in order to be together, we had to be married. A relationship of any kind outside of marriage between men and women was forbidden in our culture. I thought being married would save my soul, but it took me deeper into the blackness I was living in before. That's how my first marriage saved my soul. It took me to my darkest places and broke me. It made me question how I was living and begin to search for healing.

Two years into the marriage, my husband's company asked us to move to Tokyo. It came at a time when I was questioning my existence, and I wanted to find my purpose. It was the perfect timing. Everything was different in Japan and I was completely outside my comfort zone. I spent a lot of time alone, meditating, thinking and walking around the city, and it felt like I was in limbo. When I started to listen and get in touch with myself (from whom I was completely disconnected), I realized that I was focused on what others wanted me to be. I had thought my life was perfect and ideal because this is what the world told me it was. Yet there was a feeling of emptiness and misery that still haunted me. I didn't understand it, because I never questioned what I wanted for myself. One evening I was lying on the floor of my apartment, crying, feeling like my life was meaningless. At that moment on the floor in Japan, my 'black moment' as I call it, I was going through my darkest time and I didn't know where I was going or how to solve the mess I was in. I felt like my life was falling apart. I cried and prayed for an answer to help get me out of the misery I was living, to give me a purpose to be alive.

What followed was astonishing: an inner voice told me to park everything, and if I did I would see magic. In a week I found myself being pulled to do colour consultation training, which I stumbled upon in the *InStyle* magazine I was reading that weekend. Everything in my body told me this was what I needed to do. After that, I decided I wanted to dive deeper, so I immediately started a colour therapy diploma. It was magical. I was shown my map. This map was the beginning of my understanding of who I am, what I'm good at and my purpose in life. This map gave me plenty of defining moments: I found the courage to leave my relationship, start over and live a life that represented me. I now live a life that is purposeful, happy, full of dreams and surrounded by love.

Colour started showing up for me in the form of questions – little miracles and realizations about what was underneath my anger. The first thing that jumped out at me was my inability to wear bright colours, which brought up questions about my authenticity. To me, wearing bright colours signifies an ability to be open to and comfortable with sharing how I feel and who I am, so my fear of bright colours indicated a fear to show all of myself honestly, to listen to myself and to be comfortable expressing myself. Then, when I started to be pulled towards the colour yellow, my questions became:

Why was I creating a world full of fear and hate?
Why did I think it was OK to be treated the way I was treated?

Each moment of growth that happened over those years was like the shattering of a pair of muddy-coloured glasses, and I slowly began to see the real colours within me. The answers to these colour questions were my truth, all of me, all my feelings were heard and honoured. I cherished my mistakes as lessons, and at my core, a powerful new aspect of me grew.

I am so thankful for that 'black moment'. It held so much wisdom for me that I didn't fully understand until later. It put me on my path and made me understand my journey. This book will never ask you to neglect your black and shadowy moments. Rather, it asks you to embrace these darker parts of yourself and treat them like a child who needs listening to. I truly believe that everyone has their own path, and when they allow it to, it will show them the way, sweeping them off their feet into a world they've always known existed within.

The first time I saw through coloured glasses was the most humbling and empowering moment for me, and I hope you find some of that rebirth and magic here.

The History of Colour Therapy

Colour tells the human story. Our relationship with colour has evolved alongside our cultures, religions and lives. It is one of the most intimate relationships we have, yet we tend to take it for granted. Colours are everywhere around us, and we interact with colour all day long – through our food, clothes and spaces. From the moment we wake up, and in our dreams, colour is surrounds us.

Our interest in colour is commonly thought of as an interest in beauty, when actually it is related to our interest in the sun. The pharaohs of ancient Egypt worshipped the god Ra (the sun god), who was considered to be the most important god. When the pharaoh Akhenaten (*c.*1380–1336 BCE) decided to reform religion from a multi-god to a single-god

theology, he chose the god Aten, who was the disc of the sun. In ancient times, humans understood that the sun was essential for life. The sun gives us light and heat, warms our seas, enables plants to produce oxygen and food; without it, life on Earth would be impossible. Colour, as the manifestation of light, held divine status throughout history, playing an important part in religious history, culture and psychology and we can use these associations as a guide to work with healing and balance.

The ancient Egyptians described colour in papyruses detailing healing recipes using plant extracts. They decorated the walls of their temples in vibrant colour and used symbolic colours in art, priests' garments, charms, talismans and burial trappings. Egyptian healers wore breastplates of blue to mark their sacredness, at a time when blue ink was not easy to acquire. Similarly, blue lotus flowers were used as a magical substance to communicate with the gods, and to see visions.

In ancient Greece, specific colours symbolized universal harmony and identified the gods, goddesses and their powers. Athena, the goddess of wisdom and warfare, wore a golden robe to signify her knowledge and holiness, and Odysseus wore purple to represent the mystery of the sea. Ancient Greek priests wore scarlet robes to symbolize their bloody encounter in the Trojan war.

In the East, Buddha is represented wearing yellow or gold to symbolize his divinity and wisdom, but he also adopted robes of red when reflecting on mankind in solitary meditation. In each realm in the Buddhist Wheel of Life, a buddha is represented by a particular colour: black for the hell beings, red for the hungry ghosts, green for the animals, yellow for the humans, blue for the demi-gods and white for the gods.

The Chinese philosopher Confucius wrote extensively on colour, even making his disdain for purple known in *The Analects, Book X, Heang Tang*: 'I hate the colour purple because it confuses us for the colour red; I hate the goody-goodies because they confuse us for the virtuous people.' In Chinese culture, certain colours are treated as auspicious or inauspicious. Colours are associated with the five elements – wood, fire, earth, metal and water – and are used in the practice of feng shui and Traditional Chinese medicine. Likewise, in Judaism, the divine hues of white, purple, blue and red represent four elements – white represents the earth, purple signifies the sea, blue for the air and red for fire.

In Ayurvedic medicine, each of the seven chakras, or energy centres of the body (which align along the spine, starting at the base of the spine and moving up to the crown of the head), is associated with a colour of the visible light spectrum (see page 37). An imbalance in the chakras can result in physical illness and blockages.

In Christianity, emerald green is the symbol of the holy spirit and blue represents the Virgin Mary. Green, too, is the colour of all colours in Islam, representing prosperity, growth and abundance. *The Koran* declares that people in heaven will be clothed in green garments. Ibn Sina, a physician, astronomer, writer and one of the most significant thinkers of the Islamic Golden Age, referenced studying colour therapy in his treatments in *The Book of Healing*. Studying the effect of three colours – red, blue and yellow – on the human body, he noticed that red increased a person's fever and blood pressure, while blue helped to lower it. Yellow, he noted, reduced inflammation and pain.

In the West, the nineteenth-century physician and American Civil War general Augustus Pleasonton used blue light to cure diseases, remedy injury and improve the growth of crops and livestock. His experiments and publications influenced scientist Edwin Babbitt to develop his theories of colour healing, identifying red as a stimulant, particularly on the blood, and blue and violet as soothing and anti-inflammatory, which began what we think of as modern chromotherapy. He developed healing elixirs by irradiating water with sunlight filtered through coloured lenses, a practice of 'charging' that continues today in many alternative therapies.

In the twentieth century, the psychological benefits of colour have also been extensively explored, from Carl Jung to Dr Max Lüscher, the creator of the Lüscher colour personality test. Colour has been used extensively in the marketing and branding of products, food, public displays and interiors, in order to influence consumers and tailor environments.

As a complementary medicine, colour therapy today not only uses the theory of light's wavelengths, vibrating at different speeds and at different frequencies, to balance the body physically and emotionally, but also colour's psychological influences.

The history of colour therapy shows us that our relationship with colour began where we began. Colour has always been a part of our daily lives – we just forget how much power it has to help us heal and understand ourselves better. Colour is something we all have in common; we all relate to it in some way or another, and our emotions have been connected to colour since the beginning of time.

CHAPTER 1

How to Work with Colour

*'Colour! What a deep and mysterious
language, the language of dreams.'*

Paul Gauguin

Now let's begin your journey of colour. Please read this chapter before you do any
of the exercises in the book. There are two parts to the chapter: the first is to prepare
you for the exercises to come and the second is to give you guidelines and pointers
on working with colour and understanding the chakras (energy centres) of the body.

You will find that this is a beautiful type of therapy – subtle, yet deep. As you work
through different challenges, you may find that many unexpected feelings and
thoughts arise and you will need the tools given here, such as journaling, meditation,
visualization and mudras, to navigate them. Always make sure you are increasing your
self-care routine as you go; this will help you integrate and process your healing.

Colour is one of the greatest tools to understanding your inner world. The more I work
with colour, the more I realize just how important intuition is in order to create and
develop your own personal story, so here I will give you the basics to establish the
unique colour recipe for your life.

You Will Need

A Journal

The work we will do together will require a lot of reflection and pouring your heart out, so make sure you do it in a journal you love. Create a daily practice: when you are not answering specific questions, use different-coloured pens that you choose intuitively, based on the colour that attracts you, and write in a free-flowing, stream-of-consciousness way. Your words don't need to make sense; think of it as releasing the traffic jam of thoughts on to the pages of the journal. No one needs to read these, not even you. This practice will help you create space for healing and happiness in your life.

Self-care List

Create a self-care list of all the things you will do to nourish yourself. It could be a bath, a yoga class you enjoy, dancing, taking a nap, something that makes you feel revitalized and full of energy. As you work with colour, you will find that self-care is an essential way to show yourself love and compassion, ensuring you stay committed to changing and transforming your life.

A Timer

For some exercises, a timer comes in handy. I personally like the Insight Timer app because it has cool bell sounds and interval bells, which are useful for some meditations. Download it or alternatively use a timer on your smart phone or watch. Some of the exercises give a time range, but it is up to you and your schedule as to how much time you spend on each one.

Water

Drink lots of water and healthy liquids before and after every meditation. The healing exercises move the energy in your body around and water helps you stay balanced.

A Meditation Space

Find a place where you can feel comfortable and not be disturbed during your meditation.

Guidelines to Remember
When Working with Colour

Before you begin, please understand that even if it doesn't feel powerful in the moment, colour is 'talking' to your subconscious mind and benefitting you.

Because you are working with your subconscious state, it is important to connect with your body and feelings. The deep fears and conditioning of your mind can take some time to break and dissolve.

The only rule of this book is to trust yourself. If any exercise asks you to visualize a specific colour but your intuition shows you another, please trust your intuition. Within these pages, you'll also find the meaning for whatever colour presents itself to you.

1. You absorb colour.

We can work with colour in many ways. We absorb colour by looking at it, visualizing it, wearing it, being around it and even consuming it at the dinner table! To get as much benefit from colour as possible, I want you to work with all of these modalities. In my workshops, I ask people to visualize a certain colour and I'll light up the room with that same colour to boost the effects.

2. Like everything in life, colour has a light and a shadow side.

Each colour contains uplifting qualities, aspects that we associate as pleasant, while also possessing a shadow side, aspects that feel uncomfortable, challenging and which are normally associated with unpleasant feelings. Whenever you work with a colour, consider both sides to fully understand the lesson offered. The shadow side is not to be avoided or neglected. It's an important part of the story, since our fears drive our courage. You can't have success without failure – they live together. They're a unit, part of the same thing. Seek to converse with the whole colour, not just parts of it. When you interact with a rose pink, for example, you are not only focusing on compassion and kindness, but you are also acknowledging and interacting with the colour's qualities of dependency and lack of boundaries.

3. You rarely work with one colour at a time.

Your body, mind and soul are a combination of elements and energies. Whenever one is affected, the others are too. If one aspect is not working as it should, another has to take on the extra responsibility, overloading it with a function that it may not be built for. In this way, imbalances can occur that affect the entire system. Always be on the lookout for more than one colour.

4. The colour you dislike the most is the one you need the most.

Usually the colours we have the strongest reaction are the ones associated with painful emotions or a state of being that we are trying to avoid at all costs. I'll give you an example. When I first started using colour therapy on myself, green was a colour that I hated, and I made sure to tell everyone as much. When I stopped to question why green made me feel agitated, I journaled my heart out and I discovered it was because I was scared of being open, vulnerable and imperfect, so I closed my heart completely. I had told myself that being emotional, sensitive and vulnerable was for the weak. But I needed the colour green. My healing had to start with opening up to myself. I worked on it and now green is one of my favourite colours to interact with.

5. Visualize colours.

- Visualize yellows, oranges and red entering through your feet.

- Green in all of its shades and hues should be visualized entering the body horizontally at chest level.

- Pink should enter in a circular motion through the heart.

- Turquoise, blue, indigo, violet, magenta and gold should all enter the body through the crown of the head.

6. Work with intentions.

Your intentions are powerful, as you direct your energy and the energy of a colour when you put a specific intention into it. For example, when I decide I want to wear purple to spark creativity, I set the intention when I put it on: 'I am putting you on to boost my creativity today.' Clear intentions help you to benefit from the light and positive aspects of a colour.

7. Keep a record of how different colours affect you.

What Is a Mudra?

This book will also be using something I like to call a colour mudra.

A mudra is a hand gesture that many yogis use around the world, with each area of the hand connecting to a different part of your energy and your brain. A mudra locks and guides energy flow. The mudras here are used in combination with colour energies so that their powers are multiplied. You will see suggestions of where you can use these in combination with exercises throughout the book.

Abhaya mudra: Referred to as the 'fearlessness' mudra, this gives courage, reduces anxiety and brings balance to the body. I recommend using it with yellow visualizations. • Raise the right hand to shoulder height, bending at the elbow, palm facing outwards and the fingers upright and together.

Garuda mudra: This 'eagle' mudra cultivates openness and freedom and releases tension from the shoulders, neck and jaw. I recommend using it with blue. • With palms facing towards you, cross your right hand over your left, and link your thumbs.

Jnana mudra: Improves mental focus, memory and insight. It's useful for when you are having a hard time sitting and meditating. Use it with indigo. • Touch the tip of the index finger to the thumb, keeping the remaining three fingers lightly extended.

Kalesvara mudra: The 'womb' mudra is used to reduce anger, foster safety and release toxic patterns. I recommend using it with orange. • Interlace all fingers towards your palms, except index fingers and thumbs, then press the pads of these together and point outwards to form a diamond shape.

Kali mudra: To remove obstructions and regain positivity and courage in difficult times, this mudra helps align you to your divine power. I recommend using this with violet. • Bring your palms together, interlace your fingers, extend your index fingers and cross your thumbs.

Lotus mudra: Like a lotus that grows from underneath the mud into the most beautiful flower, this will help you align with gratitude and empathy and realize that love is the path of power. • Bring the base of the palms together, touch the thumbs and pinky fingers together, and open out the remaining fingers. I recommend using this with white and pink or lilac.

Energy Grounding

Before starting any energy work, I always recommend that you become familiar with grounding.

Grounding is a way to connect your energy body to the earth's energy. It means being present in the moment and nowhere else. When you are not grounded, you are unfocused, anxious, stressed, controlling and just all over the place. The act of grounding creates peace between your energy body (the layers of vibrating energy that make up our aura) and your physical body. It helps you focus on life from a place of love and intuition.

I find that grounding is an important basic part of each day, but we tend to neglect it. Without grounding, energy can't be released. We feel unbalanced, foggy and overwhelmed. Our boundaries can be lost; when we attempt powerful spiritual work without it, we end up flying into 'la la land' and escaping.

Grounding is essential for working with any form of energy healing. Spend time understanding and practising it. All it takes is practise, practise, practise.

I recommend that you check your grounding cord a few times a day in the beginning, and always make sure you practise the exercise before any meditation or healing work.

GROUNDING EXERCISE

1 Set your timer for 10 minutes.

2 Sit in your meditation space or on a chair, making sure your back is straight, with your palms facing downwards.

3 Start by gently closing your eyes. Bring your focus to your breath by taking five deep breaths.

4 Bring your right hand to your tailbone and bring your focus to that area; take three deep breaths and connect with the energy centre there (the base chakra, see page 37). Know that the energy in this centre is infinite. The energy is often red, but take note if you visualize another colour.

5 While breathing easily, visualize a cord pulling downwards from this energy centre. Allow your grounding cord to move further downwards, through the foundation of the building you are in, the layers of earth below you, and on down into the centre of the earth where you see a giant crystal quartz shining brightly.

6 Tie your cord around the crystal and let the energy flow from the crystal through the cord to your body, balancing and clearing it.

7 Remain in this position for the next five minutes, breathing and enjoying the present moment.

8 When the timer bell rings, take a deep breath. When you feel ready, open your eyes. If desired, repeat this affirmation to yourself: *'I have an unlimited amount of love, light and vitality that heals everything.'*

Basic Colour Meanings

We are all attracted to different colours at different periods in our lives. They are messages from our subconscious to tell us that we need a particular energy at that time. These messages don't often come with a single colour, as sometimes we are attracted to more than one colour at a time, but if it is only one colour you are responding to, that's fine too. Take note of each colour's meanings and combine them to help you understand the advice the colours are offering you. Always remember to let your intuition guide you.

On the following pages, you will learn the colours that are aligned with each of the body's seven energy centres, or chakras. Each chakra vibrates at a particular frequency and is aligned with a specific colour. If one of your chakras is blocked, you will feel unbalanced, but you will find meditations to release these blocks on the following pages. The chakras run from the base of the spine to the crown of the head: the base, or root, chakra is located at the base of the spine and is red; the sacral chakra, just below the navel, is orange; the solar plexus chakra at the diaphragm is yellow; the heart chakra at the centre of the chest is green; the throat chakra is blue; the third eye chakra, between the eyes, is indigo; and the crown chakra, above the head, is violet.

Red

The colour of vitality, strength and masculine power, red is also the colour of action, movement and goals. Red has the longest wavelength and lowest energy of all colours, on the spectrum at 655–700 nm. To me, lowest means closest to the earth.

Many people associate red with anger, blood and war – its shadow aspects, but there is more to red. It is the colour that helps remind us of the physical part of our human experience by connecting us to action, movement and passion, and it's the colour that connects us to earth and grounds us. With red, we learn to take action when things feel stuck and we are encouraged to release all of the negative energy to the earth, providing a healing exchange between us and the planet.

What a wonderful connection and acceptance we could have with our human body when we form a connection with red, allowing ourselves be supported and nourished as we connect with the earth's endless supply of vitality and love.

Red and the base chakra

Red is connected to the base chakra, which is the red energy centre in the body. It is one of the strongest but, in my opinion, the most neglected energy centre we possess. It governs the following body parts: legs, feet, bones, large intestine and teeth. Many people want to begin their spiritual journey by working with the third eye energy, which is the energy of intuitive knowing, and the spiritual aspects of seeing into the mystical and communicating with the astral plane, forgetting that in order to absorb new information from the astral plane and process our intuition, our base needs to be strong so that it is able to release energy we don't need. A strong red energy in the body keeps us grounded, safe and present in order to enjoy the experience of our physical body.

RED CHAKRA MEDITATION

1   Set your timer for five to seven minutes.

2   Sit in your meditation space, with your spine straight and your neck and shoulders relaxed.

3   Imagine a red beam of light, with incredible healing power, emerging from the earth and connecting to your base chakra.

4   Allow this light to move easily and gracefully to different parts of your body.

5   Any time the light touches a part of your body that is disturbing you, whether it feels like a physical pain or an emotional block, allow the light to dissolve it.

6   Visualize the light touching different parts of your body that need healing and repeat: *'Universe, move your healing read through my mind and body so I can return to a state of vibrant wellbeing.'*

7   When the timer bell rings, take a deep breath. When you feel ready, open your eyes.

Orange

My favourite colour to work with, orange is the colour of optimism, the colour that brings us together. It also holds the intuition and intelligence of the body – where we feel and understand things in the body. It's the power colour between red and yellow, and it vibrates on the light spectrum at 585–620 nm.

Orange helps us connect with our playful nature, our inner child, synchronicity and our mother – the mother who gave birth to us or who became our guardian. Orange helps us to become more sociable, and it represents our first relationship, our relationship with our mother. Understanding your mother's effects on you is vital to activating this part of your inner rainbow of colours. We all have a rainbow inside of us, where some colours are more dominant than others, corresponding to our personalities and soul vibrations. You will learn more about colour personalities in chapter two (see pages 70–97).

Orange also helps us to let go of anger, to embrace our feminine intuition and to get through times of grief. Orange is associated with sexuality, feminine power and it is a symbol of fertility. The lighter shades of orange, such as peach, stimulate youthfulness and our connection to the energy of grace.

Orange and the sacral chakra

This is the 'I feel' energy centre – the element of water in the body and the body's physical, mental and emotional 'flow'. The sacral chakra is located just below the navel and is the centre of creativity, joy and creation. Desire, pleasure, sexuality and procreation are the functions of this energy centre.

This area, for women specifically, is prone to being blocked, because for many reasons, both cultural and religious, women have been shamed for their sexuality throughout history. Clearing this centre can alleviate oppressive masculine energy. Clearing the obstacles to your orange energy is vital for female empowerment and success.

ORANGE CHAKRA MEDITATION

With this meditation, my intention is to have you feel the orange colour element in your body and decide what it represents for you. Concentrating on the sacral chakra, this meditation releases emotions and heals the mother connection. Practise it with the kalesvara mudra (see page 33).

1   Set your timer for five to seven minutes.

2   Sit restfully in your meditation space, making sure your back is straight and shoulders are relaxed.

3   Bring your attention to your belly and hips. Breath in and out through your nose, allowing the air to expand your belly.

4   Keep both the inhale and exhale times equal.

5   Visualize a small ball of orange light in your belly, and allow it to grow slowly, expanding with every breath.

6   Notice any feelings that arise for you. Stay here, allowing the orange colour to wash away all the heaviness from your body.

7   When your timer bell rings, return to your breath. When you feel ready, open your eyes.

Yellow

Yellow is a colour of mental strength and inner power. It's the closest colour to sunshine, and it vibrates on the light spectrum between 556–589 nm.

Yellow stimulates the mind, although too much yellow can make us anxious and lead to overthinking, especially when accompanied by black. The black-and-yellow colour combination is best when only used for a short period of time, as otherwise it can result in anxiety. Yellow is a colour that helps us find our inner sunshine – the confidence and the self-belief that comes from within, which doesn't rely on the validation of the outside world. The power that is within is infinite; it is a power that helps us see that we can be anything we want to be and achieve all our dreams. This power can be scary, because to tap into it we must first face what pains us, what scares us. These are the kind of powerful shifts we should expect when working with yellow. An attraction to yellow means that life might be throwing situations at you that challenge your inner power and bring out your fears. The universe and your soul are asking you to step up and find your inner sunshine and stand in your power.

Yellow could also be a sign that you are spending too much time in your head, thinking about the future and worrying about making mistakes, which means that you need to use meditation or other soothing techniques to help calm your thoughts.

Yellow and the solar plexus chakra

What a powerful centre this is. Also called the manipura (lustrous gem) chakra, I find it to be our most challenging chakra because it calls on us to deal with our fears, accept them, love them and embrace our inner power; an inner power that is warm, nurturing and infinite. This chakra is the centre of confidence, self-belief and inner resilience. It is connected to the stomach and upper digestive system and the muscles.

YELLOW CHAKRA MEDITATION

With this exercise, I want you to feel and understand the power of your inner sunshine, deep within yourself. Enjoy your moments with yellow – it will connect you to your strength like no other colour. You may like to practise this meditation with the abhaya mudra (see page 32).

1   Set your timer for seven to 10 minutes.

2   Sit with your spine erected and shoulders relaxed.

3   Bring your focus to your diaphragm, where your solar plexus chakra resides.

4   Focus your eyes on the tip of your nose and breathe deeply, keeping your inhale and exhale times equal.

5   Visualize sunlight glowing and expanding from your diaphragm.

6   When the timer bell rings, sit comfortably for a few breaths and, when you are ready, gently open your eyes.

Green

Before I tell you about green, I'd like to share a personal story I have with this colour. It changed my life and helped me to redefine my understanding of sensitivity, from being a weakness to being a strength. Green had always been a colour I rejected. I didn't like to wear it or be around it – I even told myself that I didn't like the mountains because of it and I only wanted to be near the sea. When I started working with colour, the first homework I was given was on green! It angered me. I didn't want to begin with this colour, but I had to. So with the yellow personality that I am (you will find yours in the next chapter), I have an attitude of all or nothing, and I was able to see that I needed to conquer my fear and beat this hatred for green.

I remember making myself sleep with green sheets and finding myself getting angrier by the day, until green revealed the reason why I was angry. It was because I believed my sensitivity and emotions were my greatest weakness and that I had to change that about myself. I was empathetic, but everyone around me, my family and my teachers, told me that this was my main issue in life – that I had too many emotions, and I was too sensitive to the feelings of others. It wasn't until I started working with green that I realized that my sensitivity was my superpower. Rather than shutting it out, as I was told to do, I learned to pay attention to my feelings. It helped me to see all of my beauty and to love myself unconditionally. Working with green taught me that living from my heart is my truest calling. It taught me that whenever I do things with love, I thrive and shine and I connect with my happiness.

Green is in the middle of the spectrum and, as such, it is the colour of balance, openness and growth. It is a colour that cleanses and balances our entire energy – emotional, physical and mental. It's a way to help you open up, grow and get in touch with unconditional love, starting with self-love and the love of others that is within us all.

Being attracted to green often signals that it's time to let go of grudges and grief and anything else you might be holding on to – such as rejection, pain and past relationships – that's keeping you from reaching your goals and growing in your life. Green invites you to open up to the world and lead with your heart. It helps you move on by letting go of the past.

Green is incredible for calming the nervous system and soothing anger and frustration. In the physical body, green is used to reduce high blood pressure, exhaustion and headaches. Green should never be used in cancerous cases, however, as its energy promotes growth.

Green and the heart chakra

The heart chakra, as I know it, is the first step towards mystical energies; the energies that connect us with the unknown in the physical plane, the energies we don't see. It is our doorway to forgiveness – of ourselves, others and situations – and it helps us fully embraces our imperfections. It helps us accept ourselves as beings of love. No matter what has happened to us, no matter what we think is wrong with us, we are loved exactly as we are, the way we came into this world. This is where the magic of who we are begins. The heart chakra governs the lungs, heart and arms and hands.

GREEN CHAKRA MEDITATION

This meditation will help reveal your heart's magic to you: the healing powers of love, openness and flow. Green has the power to heal trauma, balance the body and bring inner peace. Take note of the emotions you feel every time you do this exercise. Practise it at least once a day for four days.

1   Set the timer for 10 to 15 minutes.

2   Sit comfortably with your spine straight, yet relaxed.

3   Take five deep breaths in through the nose and out through the nose.

4   Place your left hand on your heart. Continue inhaling through your nose but now exhale through your mouth, with your lips rounded as if you were going to whistle.

5   As you breathe, connect with the rhythm of your heartbeat through your hand. Take your time.

6   Once you connect with the beating of your heart, picture a green light filling your chest and expanding horizontally from your heart, spreading out of your body and filling the entire world with beautiful green energy.

7   Stay here with the green energy until the timer bell rings. Sit comfortably for a few breaths. When you are ready, gently open your eyes.

Blue

Blue is the colour of ease, simplicity, truth and clear communication. It vibrates between 440–490 nm. This colour always asks us to show our true self, be authentic and speak truthfully, releasing all social conditioning and expectations. This includes good listening. We often feel lost in who we are because we don't allow ourselves to listen to ourselves, our feelings or what we truly want. We often hide behind the fear of disappointment and failure so that we don't even allow ourselves to wish. This colour asks us to take a step back and listen with an open mind.

Being attracted to blue is often a calling for you to be in the world as you are – speaking your truth, not anyone else's. Blue asks you to filter through the expectation of parents, friends, society and school and to listen to your inner voice with clarity.

It asks you to take a deep look at your true wants and desires. So often other people's perceptions and expectations can get in the way, and this colour calls on you to simplify how you express ourself and make it truthful and authentic.

Blue and the throat chakra

The throat chakra is located in the centre of the throat. Its function is communication, creative expression and purification. It's the symbol of truth and it is related to the neck, shoulders, ears and jaw. So whenever we feel tension in these areas of the body, we need to focus on our truth and whether we are expressing it, or if instead we are carrying other people's stories as our own burden. This chakra is all about self-expression, how we move in the world and who we choose to be. It asks us to connect to our deepest truth by looking at all the different perspectives of who we are – our 360-degree self – and not just our personality. It encourages us to look at our shadows, our pain, our interests, our passions, what brings us joy, what brings us anger, what excites us. It is not just the personality that we construct for other people, but the complexity of who we actually are. We are not simply charming or organized, there is so much to who we are than we let ourselves or others know. Knowing our '360' helps us to express our unique selves in this world beautifully.

BLUE CHAKRA MEDITATION

This is one of the first meditations I used when I started teaching colour meditation classes, because I felt as though everyone, including myself, was filled with the voices of other people rather than their own voices. I felt that working with this colour was a great start towards understanding how one's own voice can hold healing. It always has a wonderful creative effect on everyone who practised it. This is a meditation that helps us connect with our said, and unsaid, truths. There are things we dream of, we think of, and we may tell ourselves that these things are impossible, so we hide them somewhere inside because we don't feel those dreams are 'realistic' or we are afraid of disappointment. We don't let ourselves explore our hearts' desires because we are too scared – this is our untold truth.

This exercise will open up the creative expression within you, your writing and speaking, and your inner voice will become louder and stronger. This meditation will take you closer to your authentic self.

1   Set your timer for 10 to 15 minutes.

2   Sit comfortably with your spine straight but relaxed.

3   Take five deep breaths in and out through your nose. Stretch
    your arms forwards, parallel to the floor, crossing on arm over
    the other, with the right on top of the left. Then bend your elbows
    until you find a comfortable position to rest your arms, and
    gently close your eyes.

4   Focus on the centre of your throat, visualizing a blue breath
    entering your throat and awakening your inner voice. Slowly
    all the other voices will dissolve. Your voice may manifest itself
    as a memory, a word or a phrase that you need right now. Pay
    attention to the feelings of knowing, comfort and certainty that
    arise. Sometimes your inner voice will say nothing at all, and
    that means you need stillness and rest.

5   Let the sound of your inner voice grow in strength to overcome
    all other competing voices.

6   Stay here until the timer bell rings. Sit comfortably for a few
    breaths. When you are ready, gently open your eyes.

Indigo

Indigo is the state of being where dreams happen. It's the centre of imagination and visualization.

When I close my eyes and ask to see indigo, I'm always surrounded by images of my dreams, the lists of them that I wrote when I was a child. I dreamed of all the goals I would reach, and I danced to the sounds and visions of my dreams. Then adults told me that dreams were only for children and I needed to get in touch with reality. For many of us, life's disappointments, and having to be a responsible adult, holds us back from letting ourselves dream. But dreams give us hope, happiness and joy. Dreams help us achieve our desires. Losing a strong connection with indigo means we lose our ability to fly. Within us all is the ability to visualize the things we desire most and make them a reality.

Trusting in the mystery of life is vital. Working with indigo helped me to bring my dreams out of hiding and make them happen. This book in your hands right now could do that for you.

Indigo is a colour of universal wisdom, mysterious and unlimited in its power and knowledge. The colour asks us to have faith in the universe and to let go of the drama and earthly blocks that don't serve our highest purpose.

Being attracted to indigo could mean that you're spending too much time getting wrapped up in the drama of everyday life and giving in to the excuses of procrastination. The colour asks you to look for solutions, and not look at the obstacles. It asks you to dream and to trust your intuition, to allow yourself to be guided and to let go of control. Indigo is also considered to be the 'warrior' of idealism, but sometimes this warrior focuses on changing the external world and never gets anywhere, and becomes angry over why the world is so unjust. Instead, the warrior needs to champion themselves and be the change they want to see in the world. When Indigo calls you, it's asking you to give yourself justice: are you being just with yourself?

It encourages you to sit in silence and connect with yourself. Listen to the universal energy inside of you.

Indigo and the third eye chakra

Many of those on the path of spirituality call this energy centre the 'seat of the soul' and seek to open the third eye in order to gain a window into the mysterious unknown. This energy centre holds much wisdom for us. Here we may consult our soul and receive the wise answers we seek. Without being open to dreams and mysteries, we fail to connect with them. This energy centre governs the eyes, sinuses and face.

Many people seek this energy centre to the exclusion of all others, believing it's the only way into their spiritual powers. However, the third eye chakra doesn't function well without us also working on the first two chakra centres – the red and orange centres. All energies are connected, and our intuition can be found in every part of our body. The third eye specifically needs the orange centre to be strong in order for it to open and flow.

INDIGO CHAKRA MEDITATION

I want you to open the gateway to your dreams, and I want you to allow your dreams to flood in. Read the instructions for this meditation before you begin. Use relaxing music here; I recommend Tibetan singing bowl sounds or ocean waves. The meditation can be practised with the jnana mudra (see page 33).

1   Set your timer for 20 to 30 minutes.

2   Lay on your back in a comfortable position. If you fall asleep, don't worry – this is about dreams after all. If you suffer from lower back pain, place a pillow or cushion under your knees.

3   Take six deep breaths in through the nose and out through the mouth.

4   Bring your focus to the area between your eyebrows. Take ten deep breaths.

5   Keep your breaths relaxed and gentle. Close your eyes after you've taken your ten breaths.

6 Imagine yourself floating easily through an indigo space full of stars. These stars represent your dreams, goals and desires. Each one might have a combination of colours or just one colour; take note of the colours. Some stars will come to you, while others will stay far away.

7 Let your calm deep breathing and the waves of indigo space around you guide you to your stars. Look at each star and notice any memories, objects, colours or words that come to mind. Every image you see will be a message from your subconscious. You might need to practise a few times to allow your imagination to open up.

8 Stay here until the timer bell rings. Sit comfortably for a few breaths. When you are ready, gently open your eyes.

Violet

Violet is a mixture of red and blue; at 400 nm on the spectrum, it has the shortest wavelength of all the colours. Violet is a colour of creativity without boundary, uniqueness without shame or guilt. When we exercise our creativity and get in touch with new ideas, we may encounter people who are uncomfortable with these ideas. Perhaps they consider them too advanced or futuristic. Many creative people feel that they are alone because others don't support their ideas. Violet is here to open you to the full flight of your ideas and reinforce their worth and potency.

Violet is the energy of thought and divine wisdom. It represents a high calling for the soul and an acceptance of divine power. This colour helps us get in touch with our psychic centres and our spiritual gifts, such as clairessence (the intuition that we feel within) and clairvoyance. When you accept the soul experience that you came here to have, knowing that you are perfect as you are now, a being of light, you will shine through life with happiness and bliss that spreads all around you. An attraction to the colour is a call for you to explore the creativity, psychic gifts and uniqueness within and around you. Violet energy also has a strong cleansing power. The best way to use it is in the violet chakra meditation on pages 63–4.

Remember, too much violet can make you lose touch with your surroundings and your physical essence. The key here is a balance between spirituality and the human experience.

Violet and the crown chakra

The crown chakra is believed to hover just above the head. It holds divine energy and it also symbolizes the end of our human journey, encouraging us to understand the real purpose of our human experience. Many believe that the crown chakra is where we find enlightenment. It also governs the pituitary gland, the brain and nervous system. It manifests itself with divine information, innovative ideas and oneness, as in the saying by Rumi:

'You are a drop in the ocean, and you are an ocean in the drop.'

VIOLET CHAKRA MEDITATION

I recommend doing this exercise before you go to bed. The meditation can be practised in combination with the kali mudra (see page 33).

1 Set your timer for seven to 10 minutes.

2 Sit comfortably in your meditation space with your legs crossed, spine straight yet relaxed.

3 Bring your awareness to your breath. Don't try to control or change your breath, just be aware of the breath and your body, taking a couple of minutes to settle into the present moment.

4 Now close your eyes and change your breathing, inhaling for five counts and exhaling for five counts. Pay attention to whether you are holding tension in any part of your body. Wherever there is physical tension, send your breath to that spot, allowing the breath to release the tension.

5 Now imagine a circle of violet flame slowly surrounding you and getting bigger and bigger until it reaches above your head. The flame will release any blocked energy, tension or negativity, and it will burn anything that is not for your highest good.

6 Sit here until the timer bell rings, letting the violet flame cleanse your energy field completely. When ready, open your eyes.

Pastel Colours

I like to refer to these as "millennial" colours because the generation has really made an impact on the world by being more creative, more flexible and finding new ways to communicate. Millennials heralded in changes, innovations and new ways of living – and I feel that these colours are interesting to look at, to understand the meanings behind change.

First of all, these colours have one thing in common: they are tints. A tint is a mixture of a colour with white. White is the colour of fresh starts and new beginnings, but when it is paired with another colour in the spectrum it adds further meaning, giving that colour a softness and a lighter touch. All of these colours symbolize new beginnings and a new, more soulful world.

Pink and Rose Pink

This colour is a calling for self-love, self-nurturing and an unconditional loving relationship with yourself. Rose pink asks you to fall in love with yourself – meaning establishing healthy boundaries and loving yourself without conditions. Don't wait to get a better body or promotion to love and take care of yourself: just love yourself anyway, right now.

Soft Purple

These lavender and lilac tones invite you to cultivate an appreciation for the things you do and for who you are. Sometimes we focus on the next big step and forget about celebrating the small miracles that led us to the big one. This colour asks you to look for meaning and purpose with everything you do. Find your soul in your new beginnings. Pastel purples, such as lilac and lavender, can indicate a business that has soul and community at its heart – an enterprise that not only generates money but also supports ideals and high values.

Soft Yellow

Have you ever considered that the strength within you is infinite? Whether you have or not, pale yellow calls on you to cultivate that inner power by looking at your shadow side – your imperfections that make you who you are – and letting go of perfection and self-judgement. Take into consideration the fact that your flaws, your pains and what you consider to be your weaknesses are your sources of individuality. Soft yellow teaches you to be courageous with all of your parts – the dark, the light and everything in between. It's also a calling for you to believe in yourself fully. Believe in who you are, exactly as you are right now, and the value you bring into this world, by connecting to your inner sunshine (see also pages 44–6).

Pastel Green

This colour encourages growth by helping you let go of things that are no longer serving you well. People don't often think growth and loss connect, but they are two sides of the same coin. What are you holding on to that is stopping you from developing and blossoming? A past pain, a relationship gone bad, old habits? Pastel green is an invitation to let go of these things and allow yourself to flourish.

CHAPTER 2

Your Colour Personality

*'The soul becomes dyed with
the colour of its thoughts.'*

Marcus Aurelius

We all have different aspects to our personalities due to our cultural background,
life experiences and the choices we have made, but our personality is also tied to
the colour 'sign' we were born under. In this chapter you will discover how to use
numerology to decode your colour personality and learn more about yourself.

The colours associated with your birth day, month and year reveal so much about
your journey through life. The colour for your birthday reveals the essence of who you
were before you had any earthly experiences, and connecting with this colour enables
you to connect to your true self, unencumbered by external influences. For example,
if your birthday colour is yellow and you love this colour, you should find it easy to be
in sync with your essential nature, because yellow is the colour of self-belief. On the
other hand, if you feel repelled or indifferent towards your birth colour, I invite you to
connect with it more, by contemplating the feelings it brings up for you. The colour in
your birthday chart is also the best colour to use in meditation or visualization work, as
it can supercharge you and link you to your soul's purpose.

The colour associated with the month you were born represents the challenges you
are here to learn from in order to grow and develop as a person. These challenges are
a great way to see where you are in your self-development journey and can highlight
beliefs or ideas that you need to release in order to thrive.

Colour Numerology

Numerology is the study of numbers, their vibrations and their energy aspects. The relationship between numerology and colour is one of the strongest and oldest in history. The numbers here identify the wavelength and vibration of a colour in connection with your birthday. Every number has a corresponding colour vibration. I see them as best friends or lovers: they finish each other's sentences and translate for each other.

Colour vibrations are everywhere. From the day we are born, we are attached to certain colours, just like we are connected to an astrological sign. There are three main colour vibrations – your power colours – that you are born with. Once you understand these, you will also understand why you are attracted to certain colours.

Your date of birth reveals your colour story and why you are here in this life.

1   The day you were born represents the personality that you entered life with – your true self, who you are at your core, your innate talents and your innate challenges.

2   The month you were born represents the challenges you came here to face. These challenges in your environment will help you develop your talents and move you forwards. What did you come here to learn?

3   The year you were born represents the colour energy of your purpose. When you live in alignment with this vibration, you are at your happiest.

Find your colour personality by adding the numbers of your birthday together until you can reduce them to a singular number.

For example, if you were born on the 15th of the month, you'd add 1 and 5, giving you 6. This would make you an indigo personality. See below to find out your colour personality.

1 ······ Red   2 ······ Orange   3 ······ Yellow

4 ······ Green   5 ······ Blue   6 ······ Indigo

7 ······ Violet   8 ······ Magenta   9 ······ Gold

Red

Action! Action! Action!

You are a doer and a go-getter. You make things happen; you don't
like to sit around and dream. You love attention and you don't mind
working for it. Sometimes people perceive you as aggressive or bossy
but for you this is how things are done.

Red is an energy that is vital for our spiritual transformation and
nourishment; in the body it represents connection to the material
world, being grounded to the earth and having the energy to take
action. Mentally and psychologically, red represents passion, love
and letting go of painful experiences. It also helps release excessive
energy from the body.

WHEN IN BALANCE:	WHEN OUT OF BALANCE:	TO BRING INTO BALANCE:
Goal achiever, active, cheerful, wise.	Egotistical, impatient, reactive, ungrounded.	Take part in regular, challenging exercise and learn a softer approach of communication.

Hello Social Butterfly!

You just love being around people and being part of a group. You need to make sure that your circle of friends is a sensitive group though. Most importantly, make sure you truly feel your feelings, because you are all about the feels. You care about everyone around you and want to nurture everyone, so your emotions will help you tune into other people's needs.

Orange energy, combining red and yellow, is that of emotion, intuition, gut feelings, joy and warmth. Without a healthy connection to orange, you miss the link between your connection with your physical body and your personality, confidence and self-belief. Orange represents the strongest feminine energy that exists, which is the maternal connection, and when this connection is blocked, you may feel unable to trust the messages you receive from your higher self.

WHEN IN BALANCE:
Nurturing, intuitive, joyful.

WHEN OUT OF BALANCE:
Needy, emotional, a victim (for giving too much).

TO BRING INTO BALANCE:
Watersports, beach walks, regular meditation and journaling.

Orange

Yellow

You Are the Perfectionist with Big Plans!

You dream big but tend to over-think, going over plans time and again without putting them into action. You have a tendency to lose focus and worry too much. An extremely independent individual, you love being mentally stimulated; you are keen to learn new things and you also like to know a little bit about everything. Yellow is the colour that represents inner power, self-belief and courage. It can also bring up fears about yourself and your abilities.

Most people associate the colour with sunshine, and yellow can be used to shine light on fears and to give courage to acknowledge power. We all have this light within us; we just need to embrace it. It is important for you to activate this courage if you want to live a fulfilling life, where you follow your dreams and love yourself and others fearlessly. If you are a yellow, you are analytical and creative, and you need logic to be able to understand and make sense of things. You are great to be around, as you spread love and positivity.

WHEN IN BALANCE:	WHEN OUT OF BALANCE:	TO BRING INTO BALANCE:
Independent, sophisticated, great humour.	Mean, anxious, lacking in focus.	Colour breathing, yoga and enough 'alone time'.

You Are Everyone's Friend, and You Don't Judge.

People come to you for advice because you are the go-to shoulder to cry on. You're an open book to the people you trust, but it takes you time to trust others. You thrive when doing activities outdoors. You value unconditional love and see the beauty in everything. You're graceful and always know what people need from you. Because of your caring personality, you tend to have a large circle of friends.

Your relationship with plants, herbs and nature in general is your source of power, and you find inspiration and nourishment there. You innately understand the power of nature. Just like a plant, you need your roots to be strong and nourished, so symbolically water yourself by attending to your needs regularly. Building stability by growing your own seeds for self-development is key to your happiness. Learn to move organically in the world. You don't need to follow a linear path; your path is to follow the flow of your heart. Let your relationship with nature guide you.

WHEN IN BALANCE:	WHEN OUT OF BALANCE:	TO BRING INTO BALANCE:
Caring, loyal, supportive.	Holds on to grudges, envious, angry.	Doing things with love, cooking, nature walks.

Green

Blue

The Peacemaker

You were born to express yourself, which may manifest in storytelling, writing, singing, dance or fashion. You value introspection and spending time alone recharges your battery; you listen to your inner voice more than those around you. Responsible, honest and trustworthy, you always seek harmony and peace, so you have a tendency to tell people what they want to hear in order to maintain a calm environment. You are a deep thinker and need to set a time in your day or week for your inner conversations – they help you hear your own voice amidst the chaos of other voices. You keep a tight circle of friends and family and value tradition and fairness; you are a person of principles. You thrive behind the scenes and don't like to be the centre of attention. Your words are where your hidden powers are: use words to create the life you want, pay attention to how you speak and focus on your dreams, not your concerns.

WHEN IN BALANCE:	WHEN OUT OF BALANCE:	TO BRING INTO BALANCE:
Expressive, easygoing, relaxed.	Unsure of self, rigid, floaty (indecisive).	Singing, writing, chanting.

It's All about the Truth for You.

You're a walking lie detector; people's masks don't fool you, and you see right through them. Remember not to take their words to heart – what people do or say is a reflection of who they are. It's important to learn that your fight against the injustices of the world begins by being fair with yourself. Focus this power for change on yourself.

You possess incredible intuition, which means you can be relied upon to offer sound advice. With a passion for the arts, your creativity knows no bounds and you are always seeking meaning in everything you do. However living in a dreamworld and filling your mind with knowledge doesn't make up for being grounded and taking action in the real world. Check in with your physical body whenever things start to feel intense.

WHEN IN BALANCE:	WHEN OUT OF BALANCE:	TO BRING INTO BALANCE:
Perceptive, just, inspiring.	Angry, selfish, unstable (one moment you're positive, the next you're deeply wounded).	Take a course on meditation or self-reflection, also painting, creating, cardio exercise.

Indigo

Violet

Life Is Theatre!

The world you live in is beautiful, fast and movie-like. You are a dreamer and expect the outer world to respond quickly to your inner world, but you must remember to take action to make things happen. You carry so much energy and innate wisdom that sometimes the world is underwhelming for you; it is too slow.

You have a great capacity to look within but your challenge is to learn how to listen to your high and fast vibrations. You don't mind being the centre of attention on a good day – it's all part of your creative spirit. You love the mysterious part of life, and the more you allow life to deliver its unexpected gifts, the more aligned you are to your truth. You dream big and have the ability to make your dreams happen.

WHEN IN BALANCE:

Wise, creative, outgoing.

WHEN OUT OF BALANCE:

Dramatic, stressed, obsessive.

TO BRING INTO BALANCE:

Dancing, amateur theatrics or an acting class, volunteering.

The Innovator

Inventive and always in pursuit of new ideas, you're the one who creates the trend that everyone obsesses over. You are gifted at spotting the next big thing before it happens, so believe in your instinct. You're a magnet for anything original. You can never work for others unless they can recognize and nurture your individuality. Explore entrepreneurship, because that field suits your nature. You are so ahead of the curve that you may sometimes feel misunderstood, so surround yourself with creatives like yourself. You thrive around inspiring, upbeat people. When others don't match the frequency of your intensity, it can sometimes knock you off your course.

WHEN IN BALANCE:	WHEN OUT OF BALANCE:	TO BRING INTO BALANCE:
Creative, on the go, making the world a cooler place.	Needy, depressed, out of touch with yourself.	Yoga, surrounding yourself with uplifting people, believing in yourself.

Magenta

Gold

Whatever You Touch Turns to Gold!

You have a natural gift for turning ideas into a profitable reality, but be careful not to become too focused on the 'gold'. Life will hold more meaning for you if you listen to your inner wisdom and focus on the abundance you already have within. You have a tendency to be a martyr, believing that this makes you a hero or a saviour of others, but your job is to share your teachings with the world and not carry each person individually.

You are gifted with a strong visual intuition, and working with ancient symbols can awaken that part of you. You need plenty of alone time to process the world and evolve as a person. You thrive in smaller groups that don't ask you to be anything other than who you are at that moment. You have many layers – learn to love them all.

WHEN IN BALANCE:	WHEN OUT OF BALANCE:	TO BRING INTO BALANCE:
Master of manifestation, lucky, happy.	Envious, materialistic, insensitive, unlucky.	Share your work with others, teaching, working with children.

Colour Challenges Month

The month in which you were born represents the challenges you face, which will lead you to develop as a person and gain wisdom. Life's challenges help you to progress, move forwards and heal. Your month is part of your colour profile – you are a combination of your day colour and your month colour. Take a look at your month colour to see where your specific challenges lie.

JANUARY – RED

Red energy is all about learning to lead, moving forwards, material value and balancing your masculine side. If you are born in this month, you will be pushed to work on these specific challenges.

FEBRUARY – ORANGE

Orange energy is about emotions, feeling safe, being you, feminine energy, balance and learning how to connect with your feelings. You will need to learn to use your intuition and feelings to make choices.

MARCH – YELLOW

Yellow is the energy of critical thinking, your inner child, inner power and inner feelings. This energy is usually focused on finding courage and dealing with your fears. Find your sunshine by embracing your shadow.

APRIL – GREEN

Green is the energy of growth, openness, letting go and living from the heart. You will be presented with challenges that show you the limits you have imposed on yourself, which prevent you from loving yourself fully.

MAY – BLUE

Blue energy is all about learning to trust and express yourself. It's the energy of the truth. This energy will push you to get comfortable with your truth and to express yourself with more ease and self-love.

JUNE – INDIGO

Here we move into an intense energy of justice. Indigo is the energy that reveals hidden things, the lies we tell ourselves, and it prompts us towards living a life that embraces truth and the collective good.

JULY – VIOLET

This colour raises trust issues. How much do you trust the world? What are your beliefs about life? What is your energy towards the universal collective? This is a great one to test your faith in the world.

AUGUST – MAGENTA

Are the feminine and masculine energies within you balanced, or do you struggle with one but have perfected the other? August also heralds innovative ideas and the creation of a new world.

SEPTEMBER – GOLD

This energy is all about the balance and relationship between materialism and sacrifice. Do you harbour feelings of guilt about others not having enough in life? How can you balance this with your material desires?

OCTOBER – DEEP RED

Deep red is red energy multiplied. There is a lot of action and potential here, and you may find it a big challenge to embrace leadership, your masculine energy or to take action towards your dreams.

NOVEMBER – RED/ORANGE

Where is your fire within your gentle side? Are you a nurturer or a creator, and can you be both? Are you able to master your emotions and take care of (and mother) yourself?

DECEMBER – YELLOW

This is an intense colour that indicates you need to learn to shine without allowing other people, your culture or your upbringing to dim your light. Be all that you can and stand in the world, proud of yourself and of who you are.

CHAPTER 3

Love Yourself into Happiness

'Your task is not to seek for love, but merely to seek and find all the barriers within yourself that you have built against it.'

Rumi

Love is something that we all seek, every day, in all parts of our lives. We usually look for it outside of ourselves first. Of course, love does exist outside of us, but if we don't find it inside, we will never be able to recognize it, whether it is in romantic relationships, friendships, work or family. This chapter will help you find the love that is within you in order to find the love that you seek around you.

We begin with self-love. I know there are many definitions of love and self-love, but you must find your own. I found this journey difficult until I understood that self-love is a daily journey and not a destination we reach – that's when I was able to find it.

For this chapter, we're going to work with lots of different colours and combinations of colours, as well as colour breathing exercises. To get the best results, it's good to work with a few colours at the same time.

Self-love

Love is one of the most terrifying things in life – we crave it but it leaves us vulnerable. It strips us naked, exposing all our fears, fantasies, hopes and disappointments. Love carries everything we want and everything that scares us. We desire love so badly, but we seek it full of expectations and with all our protective gear on. We don't want it to have any risks or disappointments; we look for it to be perfect and to even fix us and our lives. We look for love without understanding how our life journey may have blocked us from being receptive to it. Love helps us grow and thrive, but it requires space, surrender and trust.

To find the love that we seek, we need to put aside our protective barriers. We can't approach love with our barriers up, shielded from the fear of disappointment, pain or anger. We can't ask for love when we feel undeserving of it, because we aren't at a certain weight or a certain place in life. If we want to fully experience love, we must understand that love is a journey that isn't a straight line and that we will have moments of disappointment as well as moments of pure joy. Love cannot be experienced if we are bringing along baggage from the past, rather than lessons. Loving, knowing and taking care of yourself is the key to jumping into the unknown journey of love.

The ironic thing about our barriers, or walls, is that we subconsciously use them to keep love away when we actually want to let love in. This is because we are holding on to past pain. This pain doesn't necessarily come from a lover; it could be from our childhood experiences. I have read so many self-help books that told me I needed to love myself first, in order to be loved, and that I had to stay alone for a while to recognize it and follow a set of rules. I felt bad because I didn't do that, and there was a constant block between myself and this so-called self-love. I saw my friends able to feel self-love and I couldn't. The block was so strong that it felt like a wall between myself and my belly, and breathing into my belly was difficult and frustrating. I would get angry every time I tried. So, we will begin by looking at where your walls are, and you will do work based on the location of your blocks.

Self-talking

The first thing I like to address when talking about self-love is our self-talk – the way you talk to yourself. So, alongside the block test you will find below, I want you to spend a few days noticing how you speak to yourself; how you respond to yourself, especially when you are not being the 'perfect' version of you.

Do you criticize yourself harshly?

Do you feed yourself with self-doubt?

What are the negative stories you tell yourself about you or others?

Write down your self-talking phrases in a journal and, at the end of three days, review them to see if you can find any repeating patterns.

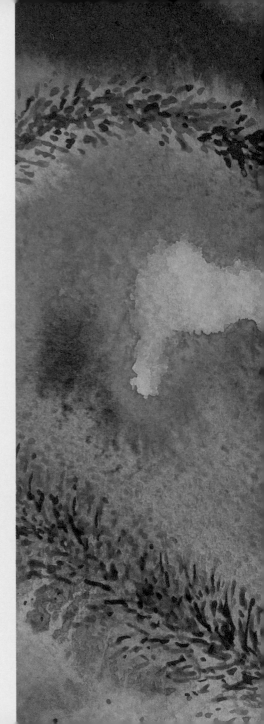

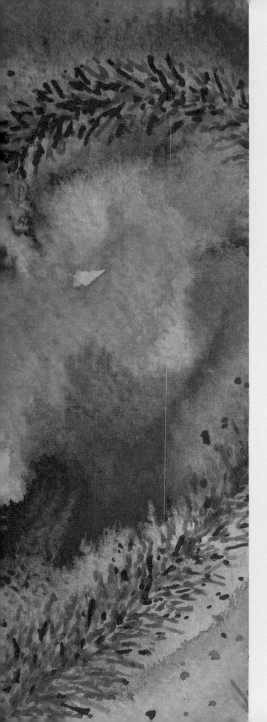

The Way You Love

For you to understand your unique way of
receiving love, why you love the way you
do and why you seek the love you do, you
must take a journey back to where you
first learned how to love – your childhood.
It doesn't need to be a long, difficult
journey; it only needs to show you what
you need to know. You can use your
journal to answer the following questions.
Looking at childhood pictures of yourself
can also help with this exercise.

> *What are your earliest memories
> of your time with your parents?*
>
> *What was the relationship between
> your parents like?*
>
> *How was the expression of love
> at home growing up?*
>
> *What did you need most from
> your parents?*

Let your pen flow with the answer to
these questions.

Are You Love Blocked?

Love blocks stop us from being fully open to love.

Often these blocks manifest in the body, in the form of pain or tension, but they can also be identified through colour breathing exercises. Sometimes the blocks are buried so deeply that you don't even realize you have them. The steps below use your breath to help you identify any blocks that you might have and help you release them. The block will feel like a pause in your breath, or a struggle in taking the breath deeper or a bit of annoyance, but often it can feel like a literal block. Once you identify the location, you will use the colour palette programmes on the following pages to release these blocks.

THE LOVE BLOCK TEST

To help you understand which colour palette holds your solutions, let's begin with a little test. You'll need a timer and a space where you won't be disturbed.

1   Set your timer for seven minutes (with the first bell to ring after three minutes).

2   Lay comfortably on your back with your palms facing the ceiling and your body relaxed.

3   Close your eyes and lay silently, without music.

4   Begin taking soft natural breaths, focusing on the sound of your breath.

5   Ground yourself by noticing where your body touches the surface underneath you.

6   Focus on breathing softly until the three-minute bell rings.

7   What colour comes to mind when you think of romantic love? If it's a pale pink, this means the love you seek is soft, compassionate and pure. If it's red, the love you're seeking is passionate, intense, strong and grounded; you could also be seeking lust.

8 Start breathing deeper into your belly, filling your entire body, visualizing your love colour expanding inside you. Notice where you feel a bit of pause in the breath or a challenge to taking the breath deeper. The breathing blocks may take time to reveal themselves. If you are new to looking for blocks in your body, you will need to relax and focus, so you can become aware of them as they slowly arise and become apparent.

9 When you are finished with this test, take a few deep breaths. When you feel ready, open your eyes.

- If the breath block is in your lower belly, work with colour palette one: pastel yellow and orange healing.

- If the block is in the centre of your torso, between your belly and your chest, use colour palette two: violet and sun yellow.

- If the block is in your chest area, work with colour palette three: pink, pastel green and bronze.

If you have blocks in more than one area, that's not a problem – you need to know that you are being asked to go deep and bring all your power out beautifully, so start with the belly palette.

Belly blocks

We usually hold on to anger and frustration in this area. The belly can often store grief, old traumas and painful experiences that we haven't dealt with or acknowledged. This block is usually related to the mother wound; blocks that originate from the mother, either by how she treated you or how she let herself be treated. Mother wounds are often challenging to acknowledge because we may feel that if we look at our parents' negative aspects, then we are in some way betraying them – but that isn't the case here. This can be a sign that you weren't made to feel emotionally safe as an infant, or your parents tended to your physical needs but not your emotional ones. If you had any emotional, physical or sexual abuse, it can manifest itself here. You may not feel nurtured emotionally or sexually by yourself or others. This area usually needs a combination of colours to promote emotional safety and trust in oneself.

Diaphragm blocks

This block indicates that you re stuck in the powerful 'victim circle', as I like to call it. It's a cycle that happens when you know you have the power to take charge of your life, but you are either afraid to take action or you don't want to. It's an interesting cycle. It's usually hard for you to let go of struggles – past or present. You sometimes seek struggle because you believe that you deserve it. It's hard for you to see that you are choosing these experiences for yourself. You play a part in rejecting your imperfections, you ignore your fears and you don't take responsibility for your life. You are the creator of your own block, like no other. This cycle comes from the fear of not being perfect, and you feel that if you admit your mistakes, then you are doomed. You have the courage and the clarity within you to break this cycle. That power is inside of you.

Chest blocks

A block found in the chest is often manifested by a fear of the unknown and a fear of living with an open heart. You feel as if love has betrayed you or that you are not deserving of love because you've been mistreated before. Chest heaviness is an indication that you like to control situations, instead of allowing them to grow naturally, because of the fear of the outcome. You confuse your unconditional love and forgiveness with having poor boundaries and allowing people to walk all over you. These messages need to be redefined.

Now let us begin the healing… remember that pain is better released from the body than held in.

Colour Palette One: Yellow and Orange

This therapy plan focuses on the belly block, which is usually a deep block that has accumulated during childhood or over a long period of time. Most likely it's a result of something you decided to bury for one reason or another.

For the next ten days, these two colours will be your friends. You will be using them for the healing process, so surround yourself with them, wear them, use them as a wallpaper on your phone, eat foods in these colours and practise the exercises below.

The exercises are accompanied by questions that you can reflect on in your journal. Before you begin the exercises, turn the page and read the questions without answering them. This will help the answers arise naturally during the exercises.

Days One to Four

The daily yellow clearing exercise (see page 11) reveals the blocks that you have stored deep down. You will be bringing all that is blocked to the surface and journaling your feelings – the first step to healing is awareness. Also, remember the self-care list (see page 26), which is useful now, as you'll need to give yourself extra love for the duration of the exercise. As you work on healing, you will encounter painful emotions that might resurface in order for them to leave your body. Your time in this practice will focus on what no longer serves you, and your time with yourself will be filled with self-loving practices. If you need a reminder or haven't made the list yet, go back and do it now.

After you do the exercise, journal your feelings. Write whatever comes to mind for at least five minutes after every daily exercise. Keeping a journal of how you feel over the four days will help you see what progress you're making.

YELLOW CLEARING EXERCISE

1   Set your timer for 15 minutes.

2   In your meditation space, sit in a comfortable position,
     alert yet relaxed.

3   Take three deep breaths in through your nose and out through
     your nose.

4   Bring your right hand to your belly. Let it hover just in front of
     your body without touching. Let your left hand rest comfortably
     on your lap with your palm facing the ceiling.

5   Visualize a glowing yellow light forming in your right hand and
     radiating out from it. Envision it getting stronger with every breath.
     Let the light shine on your belly and fill it with yellow energy.

6   During this visualization and breathing you might notice
     emotions and uncomfortable feelings. These are the blocks.
     When this comes up, deepen your breath and allow the yellow to
     start melting the fortresses inside you, opening shut boxes and
     allowing you to feel all you need to feel to release it.

7   Whenever you feel distracted, bring your attention back to your
     breath and the feeling of yellow light filling your belly.

8   Once the timer bell rings, release your hands and bring your
     breathing back to a natural relaxed pace. When you feel ready,
     open your eyes and start journaling. Let your pen flow.

Days Five to Ten

The next six days will focus on orange healing energy and you may find you experience big releases of anger, frustration and hidden emotions during these exercises. After these feelings are released, the orange energy of joy, intuition, nurturing and femininity will become stronger in your body. You will feel more open to receiving love and manifesting it. Enjoy the release and the joy that will follow.

ORANGE HEALING EXERCISE

1 Set your timer for 15 minutes (with an interval bell at seven minutes).

2 In your meditation space, sit in a comfortable position, alert yet relaxed, with your eyes closed.

3 Take five deep breaths in through your nose and out through your mouth.

4 Imagine an orange ball in your belly, starting from a small dot that grows slowly with every breath you take. See the ball filling your belly.

5 At the seven-minute bell, change your breathing to three short inhales through the nose and one long exhale through the mouth. This cycle of breathing is one round. After five rounds of breathing, take your right palm and tap the top of your head five times. Repeat the five rounds until the timer goes off.

6 After the timer bell rings, go back to breathing normally. Sit for a few minutes. When you feel ready, open your eyes.

Reflection Questions

Complete the questions below after your meditation.
I recommend you do it after the third day.

Am I allowed to be angry? What's underneath it?

What do I need from myself to feel nourished?

Who am I without my sadness and anger?

Colour Palette Two: Violet and Yellow

This plan focuses on the diaphragm block, which prevents you from fully grasping your potential. When the block is released, you are able to tap into courage that you never knew existed, helping you accept your fears as an important part of who you are and to see that there is a well of infinite self-belief within you. The exercises will bring out that inner strength and independence. They will also help you embrace love and accept yourself, knowing that you are deserving of everything you wish for.

This will be a seven-day journey, so over the next week, let yellow and violet be your friends. You will be using these colours for the healing process, so surround yourself with them, wear them, use them as a wallpaper on your phone and eat foods in these colours. They will also be accompanied by questions to reflect on in your journal.

Days One to Three

You will begin with the violet swords cleansing exercise on the next page, repeated every day for three days, which will clear the blocks that stop you from recognizing your own powers. The exercise will remove any heavy energy to help you feel rejuvenated. Violet is a powerful cleanser and you will feel the effects instantly. You can use this clearing exercise whenever you feel depleted or when you've been in contact with a lot of people and feel heavy or dragged down afterwards.

VIOLET SWORDS EXERCISE

Before you begin this exercise, pick up your journal, do a quick body scan and write down how you are feeling in your physical body and your emotions. If you like, practise this exercise while performing kali mudra (see page 33).

1   Set your timer for 10 to 15 minutes.

2   In your meditation space, sit in a comfortable position, alert yet relaxed, with your eyes closed.

3   Take deep breaths in through your nose and out through your mouth, throughout the entire exercise.

4   Become present in your body, allowing your body to relax with every breath you release from your mouth.

5 Focus on your diaphragm. Visualize violet flaming swords surrounding you in a circle, with the swords releasing energy from you in black smoke. The swords will only release and burn off the energy that is not connected to the high frequencies of love and gratitude.

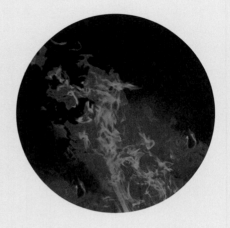

6 After the flaming swords clear away the energies around your body, visualize the swords spinning around you in a circle, creating a violet tornado, which will clear your body from head to toe, leaving your energy vibrant, clear and sparkly again.

7 After the timer bell rings, bring your attention back to your breathing, returning to the natural rhythm of inhaling and exhaling through the nose.

8 When you feel ready, open your eyes, pick up your journal and write freely about how you are feeling emotionally and in your physical body.

Days Four to Seven

This yellow exercise will help strengthen the power of your own voice that is within you. This voice will help you understand that your fears are part of you, and that courage and strength don't mean a lack of fear or vulnerability. By the end of this exercise, you will feel as though you can do anything, that you can love fearlessly and open yourself up to others.

SUNSHINE YELLOW EXERCISE

1 Set your timer for 15 minutes (with an interval bell at 12 minutes).

2 Sit restfully in your meditation space. Bring your right hand in front of your chest, at the same level as your heart, facing outwards in abhaya mudra (see page 32).

3 Place your left hand on your lap facing upwards.

4 Close your eyes and bring your focus to your breathing. Take three deep breaths and release – release your day, your to-do list and be one with your breathing.

5 Start breathing in through your mouth and out through your mouth. Continue throughout the exercise.

6 Now bring your focus to your inner sun, wherever you feel that is located. Is it shining brightly or is something blocking it? If there is a block, what is it? Specific words, feelings or memories might arise.

7 Imagine breathing in bright yellow through your nostrils, letting it grow inside of you with every breath and break away any blockages or shadows that are dimming your inner sun and stopping it from shining brightly.

8   Let the yellow sunshine within you grow and visualize it shining through your right hand. Breathe in courage, fearlessness and confidence, and as your sun shines brighter you will start seeing your beauty more clearly.

9   At the 12-minute bell, release the mudra and release the yellow.

10   Sit restfully, breathing in through your nose and out through your nose until the last bell rings.

11   Slowly move your fingers and your toes. When you are ready, open your eyes, then turn to your journal and start writing.

Reflection Questions

What is vulnerability to you?

What is courage to you?

What can you do today to feel more courageous in your life?

Colour Palette Three: Pink, Green and Bronze

A chest block is one of the most common blocks, usually manifesting itself as neck and shoulder pain. It originates from past hurt or the belief that there are too many conditions necessary for you to be lovable. This block also forms when we don't forgive ourselves for mistakes that we made in past relationships, or from the fear of being vulnerable and open. When healed, you feel free and strong. Clearing the chest block is essential for self-love to freely manifest and become part of your daily existence.

For seven days, pink, green and bronze colours will be your friends. Surround yourself with these colours, wear them, use them as a wallpaper on your phone, eat foods in these colours and do the exercises on the following pages. The exercises are accompanied by questions for you to reflect on in your journal and the journaling should be done *before* the exercises, rather than after. The first exercise will help you open yourself to your soul in order to heal, and the second is to help you establish personal boundaries.

Days One to Four

The first part of the energy healing exercises uses pink and green colours, which will open up your energy for divine healing from the soul. We are going to use the power of love to heal and release blocks because the soul heals with love. You will find that you are made of love, you are loved unconditionally and that you can love unconditionally.

Reflection Questions

Answer these questions before you start the bliss exercise.

Love is...

Write a minimum of ten statements.
This will reveal how you define love.
Make sure you are honest;
include the negative as well as the
positive beliefs you have about love.

Where in my life can I let myself
receive more love?

PINK AND GREEN BLISS EXERCISE

1   Set your timer for 15 minutes (with an interval bell at
    six minutes).

2   In your meditation space, sit in a comfortable position, alert
    yet relaxed. Rest your hands in your lap, palms facing upwards.

3   Take three deep breaths in through your nose and out through
    your nose, and settle down into your body. Clear your mind of
    any worries or things you have to do, and allow yourself to be
    present in the moment. Close your eyes and shift your breathing
    to fill the full breadth of your lungs.

4   As you inhale, imagine a band of pink and green light glowing
    horizontally across your chest.

5   Now visualize both colours travelling to the palms of your hands
    until you feel the energy of the colours touching your palms.

6   Open your hands wider and bring them to your chest and tap
    your chest, hold for one second and repeat the words 'I am love'.
    Feel the pink and green energy filling your entire body. Then
    open your arms wide out to both sides.

7   Feel your chest opening and releasing all that no longer serves
    you. Repeat until the first timer bell rings.

8   After the first bell rings, place your hands on your lap, palms facing upwards.

9   Take three deep breaths. When you feel ready, open your eyes and begin journaling for at least five minutes. Let your pen flow, describing how you felt and what thoughts, sensations or emotions arose for you during the visualization.

Repeat the exercise and journaling daily to track the progress you are making.

Days Five to Seven

Blocks in the chest usually mean that we don't have good boundaries. The best definition of boundaries is Brene Brown's in her book *Rising Strong* where she says:

> *'Boundaries are simply our lists of what's okay and what's not okay. It's so straightforward and it makes sense for all ages in all situations. When we combine the courage to make clear what works for us, and what doesn't, with the compassion to assume people are doing their best, our lives change.'*

Many of us confuse being kind and loving with giving beyond our capacity, believing that saying 'no' to something that doesn't work for us makes us bad people. Another reason for this is because we base our likeability on others. When we start working on self-love, we find the ability to love ourselves without needing validation from others. Setting boundaries is important in our work towards self-love. It helps us to stay compassionate without the resentment we feel when we say 'yes' to something when we really want to say 'no'.

Reflection Questions

Answer these questions before you start the bronze boundaries exercise.

How do I define boundaries?

Where do I need boundaries the most in my life?

What will happen in my life when I start saying no to the things I don't want to do? Or can't do?

What are the small steps I can take to enforce my boundaries?

LOVE YOURSELF INTO HAPPINESS

BRONZE BOUNDARIES

It's important to define boundaries for yourself and know where and when you need them. Take this one step at a time. Start small.

1   Set the timer to 15 minutes (with an interval at three minutes).

2   Stand in your meditation space, making sure you have enough room and that your floor is clear of any obstacles.

3   Start by shaking your hands and shoulders. Do little jumps and move your legs and hips for the first three minutes; if you are unable to jump, shaking your body is great. This movement can be done with your eyes open, focusing on being present in the moment. Enjoy the movement and let your body guide you.

4   After the first bell, come to a complete stop. Connect to your body by noticing the blood flow and feel your breath return to its natural rhythm.

5   A big energy release occurs after the first two steps, so notice it. This exercise will help you feel lighter and softer. Bring your breathing back to a long, soft, gentle inhale and exhale.

6   As you stand, visualize a bronze light stirring at your feet and growing. It might feel like heat or a tingling; if you don't feel something the first time, don't worry – your intention is enough.

7 Once the bronze light feels strong and powerful at your feet, begin walking slowly in a circle and repeat out loud the answers to your reflection questions – repeat the boundaries you need in your life, one by one and in detail, until you say them all.

8 When you finish reciting your whole list of boundaries, say 'So it is', and close the boundary circle by returning to the standing position where you started.

9 Take a few deep breaths. When you are ready, clap your hands and leave the circle. The clap will signify to your body that this energy exercise has ended.

Colours of Forgiveness

Forgiveness is an essential part of finding love within yourself and for attracting the love that you seek from others. Any unforgiveness or grudges that you hold on to from the past act as blocks to the high-vibration love you desire.

Unforgiveness, anger and resentment are undesirable attitudes and emotions we don't choose to have but, at one time or another, we all do, and they often result in poor behaviour. Why is this? On some level, we believe this anger serves and protects us; we often have a hard time forgiving and letting go because we believe that when we do, we lose the lessons we learned from the challenging situations we experienced. When we forgive, we may believe it makes the way that people treated us acceptable, but this is not true. When we forgive someone who has hurt us, we may believe we need to let that person back into our lives. But forgiving them doesn't mean they are permitted to be in our life.

In this section, I will guide you through a colour forgiveness exercise that will open the doors of your heart wide. The best description of forgiveness I've heard comes from Maya Angelou in a conversation with Oprah Winfrey, and it is exactly what we all need in this process:

> *'When you forgive somebody, it doesn't mean that you invite them to your table; it means I'm finished with you, we have to be able to protect ourselves.'*

'Finished' here also means I'm finished with the pain you caused me. I give it away, I learned the lesson and I no longer need to carry the pain with me.

Forgiveness of others is important, but it's nothing compared to how much we need to forgive ourselves because when we neglect to practise self-forgiveness, we punish ourselves instead. We tend to subconsciously disallow good things to come to us because we feel we need to be punished for the mistakes we made. Anger towards ourselves comes from deep within, and makes us feel undeserving of things such as love, success or happiness. We tend to bury this unforgiveness so deep that we don't realize that we have it.

FORGIVENESS EXERCISE

You'll need to be comfortable during this exercise as you'll be spending an hour here. You will also need your journal and a green pen.

1   Set your timer for one hour with an interval bell at 15 minutes.

2   Sit comfortably in your meditation space, or any space that you chose. I usually recommend doing this exercise in nature outdoors, but your favourite meditation spot is perfect too. Wherever you choose to do this, set the mood and be comfortable and undisturbed for at least an hour.

3   Write down the names of the people that have hurt you. The hurt can be small or big – write it all down. Also, add situations or incidents and don't forget to add yourself into the scenario too. Take as much time as you need.

4   Take a last look at all these names and all these situations, then rip the paper into small pieces.

5   Check your timer is set for a remaining 30 to 45 minutes.

6   Sit comfortably or lay down, whichever feels right for you, then take seven deep breaths in through your nose and out through your mouth, relaxing into your position.

7   Visualize yourself on top of a mountain, sitting on a golden throne. This is the throne of your life – you are the king or queen of your life, remember. Pardons are only given by kings and queens.

8   Visualize all these hurtful people and situations that you have written down standing in a queue, all coming to ask for forgiveness. Each time one of them comes to you, repeat this statement: 'I forgive you, thank you for the lesson, now leave with love.' Repeat this until each person or situation disappears or turns into light.

9   Now imagine wrapping yourself in a green silk robe, allowing all the forgiveness work that you have done today to leave your body to create space for more love, more compassion and more high-vibration love in both people and situations.

10   After the timer rings, take a few deep breaths and give yourself a hug. When you're ready, open your eyes.

You might need to do this exercise more than once. This exercise will show you that you don't need to be angry because it takes so much effort to hold on to anger and resentment. Forgiveness is the way to feel lighter and more open.

Colours of Attraction

Attractiveness is something that comes from within. It's a combination of how we feel about ourselves and the image we project to the outside world. We often struggle with feeling attractive and accepting ourselves if we don't meet the unachievable levels of perfection that society imposes on us. It's no wonder we fail to see our own beauty when it falls outside such narrow definitions. Overwhelmed, we often don't allow ourselves to see who we are in our own truth. Our imperfections, the very things that cause us shame, are what makes us unique and can be the foundation of our beauty.

This exercise is all about revealing the beauty within,
and even if you don't believe it, colour will project the truth.

Commit to this short exercise at least once a week and you'll begin to see results. You will hear more compliments, people will be attracted to you, and if you are looking to date, this will benefit you in attracting compassionate people into your life.

PEACH ATTRACTION EXERCISE

For this exercise, you will need a mirror and some time with yourself.

1   Set your timer for 10 minutes.

2   Stand in front of a mirror, preferably in the morning, and look directly into your eyes.

3   Take five slow, deep breaths in through your nose and out through your nose.

4   Close your eyes and say softly 'I see beauty'. Visualize painting the phrase in a peach colour, then move that phrase to the crown of your head. Visualize the words and the colour entering your body from the top of your head, filling you with a peach hue.

5   This colour is naturally calming and will bring out your playful side. It will also make you feel more beautiful and joyous in your physical body. Repeat the first three steps three times.

6   Now visualize pulling a beam of magenta colour from the sky. Magenta has strong magnetic energy, so feel this as strong pulses of energy. Visualize the colour filling your body and projecting outwards through your face and the front of your body. Keep this visualization for a couple of minutes.

7   Open your eyes and say 'I see beauty' three times.

Feeling attractive is something that comes from within yourself. The more you practise seeing the beauty within, the more you will feel it in your whole body, inside and out.

Colours of Friendship

Friendships are the most beautiful form of energy interactions that we experience; they are filled with lessons of giving, receiving, love, pain and much more. Friendships can take many forms; some friendships teach us lessons, while others are there to accompany us on this beautiful journey we call life – it is important to understand the difference between these. We attract friends for various reasons; some friends show up at a certain time for a particular purpose.

The universe supports us by bringing friends into our life, often to help take us from point A to B, even if that experience is painful. Other friends come as messengers to show you what's working, or not, in your life; they act as mirrors. These messengers must be respected.

I understand many people struggle to find friends, keep friends or with friendships in general. We tend to subscribe to what social media shows us about friends, forgetting that we have a role in attracting what we want.

The exercise on the facing page can help you cultivate more friendships and gather more beautiful energies around you. Remember, we are all travellers on this journey, and when travelling we tend to make unexpected stops along the way: some of these stops include friends who redirect or affirm our paths.

FRIENDS FROM THE RAINBOW

Because we attract friendships at different times in
diverse situations, friends are like a rainbow. Each
one might come from their own walk of life and have their own lesson
to share with us. This exercise will help you attract a variety of friends
and surround yourself with loving and supportive people. You will
begin with a writing exercise.

You will need: coloured pens, paper and an envelope.

1 Set your timer for 30 minutes.

2 Use your intuition to choose a coloured pen that represents the
   friends you are seeking to attract.

3 With this coloured pen, write a letter to your new friends. In this
   letter, describe how you interact with them, what your friendship
   feels like, how you connect to each other and everything you
   want from the friendship. It's very important to know and to be
   specific about who you want to attract. Practise manifestation
   clarity: the clearer the energy you put out, the clearer the results
   you will receive.

4 Set your timer for 15 minutes.

5 Be seated or stand, whichever feels right for you. Use your breath to bring yourself into the present moment, slowing it down and focusing on it, letting your entire body relax.

6 Take the letter that you wrote in your hand and bring it close to your heart chakra centre. Close your eyes.

7 Visualize your heart centre flooding the letter with golden light.

8 Then envision the colours of the rainbow surrounding you in a circle, one by one, starting with violet, then indigo, blue, green, yellow, orange and red. Let these colours form separate concentric circles around you.

9 Visualize sending this letter into the sky and then see it break into rainbow colours and fall over the entire planet – it will attract your desires to you from all over the world.

10 Take a deep breath in, and open your eyes. Seal your letter and put it away somewhere safe.

Side note: Items we store away tend to resurface whenever we need them. If you come across the letter unexpectedly, pay attention to what it is telling you.

PINK GRATITUDE

Gratitude energy has one of the highest frequencies when it comes to emotions. When we are connected to this energy, we instantly attract synchronicity, loving experiences and more of what makes us happy. I'm bringing you this pink gratitude exercise to help you release painful experiences and encourage beautiful things into your life. I believe this energy will help you to attract the love you seek.

1   Set your timer for 10 to 15 minutes.

2   Find a comfortable seated position and close your eyes.

3   Take three deep breaths and with every breath go deeper inside, letting go of your to-do list and your worries. Centre yourself in the moment, using your breath.

4   When you feel relaxed and present, bring your attention to your heart and feel the steady pulse in your chest. Take a few moments to quieten your mind and connect with your heartbeat (place your right hand over your heart or a first finger on your wrist to help connect to your heartbeat).

5   Visualize a rose pink light emerging from your heart and shining brighter with every pulse. It fills your body with rose pink rays and fills you with universal love – the kind of love you feel when

you remember a child's laugh or when a baby smiles for the first time. This love isn't just visiting, it's always within you; you can access it any time. You can end the exercise here or take it further with the following steps.

6   To progress with this practice, send these rays of pink colour to someone you love or to the one you want to attract. To do this, visualize forming the rays into a pink ball in front of your body and filling it with the energy of love, bliss and all the things you want to attract.

7   Visualize sending the ball up into the sky so it can bring back all the things you are looking for.

8   Alternatively, you can intend this ball for yourself. Instead of sending it up to the sky, send it back into your body with all the wishes and good energy you wanted for another, but for yourself.

9   Gently release the pink ball and reconnect with your physical body. Come back to the room you are in and gently open your eyes. Take the love you felt here with you wherever you go today.

Colour Hack for a Painful Break-up

Separations are hard, whether it's with a lover, a friend or a family member. Healing is necessary and colour can help speed up the therapeutic process by using a series of exercises.

The essential part of getting over a break-up is to first allow yourself to go through it. We often try to escape from the pain, but I have found it effective to work with colours as we heal because we don't need to necessarily name the emotion or go deeper into the experience. We can gently remove the pain from the experience by connecting with the colour.

When healing from the breakdown of my marriage, it was vital for me to go within myself, reflect and understand the lessons I learned. I worked with two main colours: orange and navy blue. My closet was screaming these colours at me. I was buying them without realizing how much of them I had. I called them 'break-up colours', but later I discovered that they are often the colours that other people are attracted to after a break-up as well. When someone comes to me for a colour reading and says they're currently attracted to these two colours, I'll ask if they are going through some kind of break-up. And almost 90 per cent of the time the answer is 'Yes! How did you know?'.

These colours hold the code for healing from a break-up. The orange asks us to release the emotions we have inside, grieve and allow ourselves to fall in love with life again. Navy blue invites us to apply discipline, enjoy a time of reflection and to trust in the world again.

These two colours hold a beautiful message for all of us, especially during the times when we feel pain.

The healing plan consists of:

- Three days of the orange meditation (see pages 144–5) and reflection questions (see page 148).

- Three days of the navy blue meditation (see pages 146–7).

- The forgiveness exercise (see page 132).

ORANGE BREAK-UP RELEASE EXERCISE

1 Set your timer for 15 to 20 minutes.

2 Sit restfully in your meditation space.

3 Interlace all fingers towards your palms, in the kalesvara mudra (see page 33). This mudra might make you feel restless or impatient – if you have maternal blockages (see love blockages, pages 104–7), anger or grief, try deepening your breathing and making space for the uncomfortable emotions.

4 Keep your spine straight, close your eyes and focus on your breath.

5 Take five deep breaths. Breath here is soft and natural – inhale through your nose and exhale through your nose.

6 Visualize an orange light entering your body through your nose and travelling down into your belly, clearing all blockages that stop you from expressing your emotions on the way.

7 As the light moves around, feel yourself letting everything go: worries, anger, grief, betrayal or any other emotions that are arising.

8 Picture the orange energy as flowing water, circling in your belly like a washing machine.

9 Inhale through your nose and exhale through your mouth, knowing that with every exhale you are releasing all the pain that's in your body from this break-up.

10 When the timer bell rings, take your breath back to its natural state and release the mudra. When you feel ready, open your eyes.

11 Begin journaling for at least five minutes. Let your pen flow, describing how you felt and what thoughts arose for you during the exercise.

NAVY BLUE VISUALIZATION

Every experience we have holds lessons; we only need to allow ourselves to be open to these lessons so that we can move forwards and expand. For the next four days focus on being open, allow yourself to expand and fly.

1   Before you begin, write a set of questions about the break-up. What am to learn from this? What should my next steps be? And any other questions that you are seeking answers to. Always remember that your inner soul will answer what you need, so trust it. You can use these questions throughout the four days and elaborate on them or write new ones every time.

2   Set your timer for 15 minutes.

3   Sit restfully in your meditation space, with your back straight, yet relaxed. Rest your hands on your lap with palms facing upwards.

4   Keep your head straight and roll your eyes inwards to look in between your eyebrows. Take five slow, deep breaths in through the nose and out through the mouth with an 'Ahh' sound.

5   Gently close your eyes.

6 Visualize a beautiful navy blue spiral of light entering your body at the point between your eyebrows and filling your body with lessons from your soul. Stay here, and as soon as you hear the timer bell, take a few deep breaths, then open your eyes.

7 Pick up your journal and start answering the questions or write what you felt or visualized. Your answers will be there.

Reflection Questions

These are important questions to ask yourself whenever any relationship ends. It can be uncomfortable to look at the mistakes we made, but only when we look at these mistakes can we change things for the better. Use a light blue pen to answer these questions. Blue is a colour that is relaxing and easy and reminds us to relax during uncomfortable situations.

What is my biggest take from this relationship?

What was my part in this break-up?

What could have I done better? For myself and the other person?

Were there any red flags that I chose to ignore? Why did I ignore them?

When you are finished answering these questions, take a moment and place your hands on your heart. Fill your heart with pink and repeat three times:

'Even though this break-up happened, and I don't feel my best right now, I fully and unconditionally love, forgive and accept myself.'

CHAPTER 4

Work & Career

*'I found I could say things with colour and shapes that
I couldn't say any other way.'*

Georgia O'Keeffe

Work can be a source of pleasure or a source of stress and anxiety. When we are connected to the purpose of what we do, it becomes a source of joy. When I found my vocation in colour therapy, I discovered that I could release my fears and anxieties faster when I focused on my intention and why I do what I do. The reason behind my career choice kept me going throughout life's many challenges and enabled me to find peace and balance.

When we are connected to our 'why' and to the deeper meaning of what we do on a daily basis, it can create a wonderful life experience for us and stimulate us to do our best work. This is why the chapter begins with an exercise on using colour to connect to your inner calling. By listening to your soul, you will know how to connect your true self to the work you choose to do.

Also included here is an exercise on how to release a creative block, whether you are trying to invent something new or find a solution to a challenge at work, and exercises on dealing with procrastination and attracting abundance. Finally, there are ideas for using colour in your wardrobe to help you attain success at work.

Find Your Calling

I truly believe that we are born with our calling inside of us. The usual mistake we make is that we believe everyone's calling is a direct path, containing one passion. Indeed, for some, the passion and calling is clear from childhood, but for others, it's a combination of these things at different points in their lives. Passion, purpose or calling, whichever word feels right for you, is something personal and it's like everything in life: it's a journey, never a destination.

Looking into our childhood for clues is the best way to lead us to our calling. So let's go on a journey within, and have a little chat with your inner genius.

FIND YOUR CALLING EXERCISE

For this exercise, don't set a timer, but record yourself reciting the steps calmly and softly, then play them with some relaxing music in the background. Your voice holds power.

1   Lay down on the floor, or wherever is comfortable for you. Don't use the bed as you might fall asleep. It's acceptable for other exercises, but for this one you need to be awake.

2   Take a deep breath in through your nose and out through your mouth. Concentrate on where your body touches the surface you are laying on. Allow this surface to hold you: relax your body and give in to the support underneath you. Close your eyes and deepen your breath. Let your body become completely relaxed. Let go...

3   Breathe in for five counts and breathe out for six. Repeat for five rounds.

4   Focus your attention on your diaphragm. Visualize a yellow door opening into a beautiful path and let yourself walk through the door and down the path until you reach a little house.

5   When you are ready, enter the house and walk into a room. Take note of what is inside: the colours, the furniture and the feelings you have. Imagine yourself as a child in the room. If you have trouble doing this, open your eyes and look down at your feet, which will help you to see your inner child. Interact with this child and ask them what you came here to learn:

Why did I come into this world? What do I need?

What brings me happiness?

6   Take your time and let your experience be what it needs to be. When you feel you are finished, give your inner child a hug. Open your eyes and write down everything you saw.

Overcome a Creative Block

Creative blocks can happen for so many reasons, and some stem from our fears. The most common creativity block is authentic expression, and that is what we will work on here. For this, we will use sapphire blue, as it has tremendous healing and unlocking powers. The colour also calms the mind and the nervous system and helps relieve anxiety.

SAPPHIRE WATERFALL EXERCISE

1   Set your timer for seven minutes.

2   Settle into your seated position, close your eyes and take a couple of deep breaths.

3   Centre yourself by being one with your breath – inhaling and exhaling slowly through the nose.

4   Visualize yourself under a sapphire waterfall. The waterfall is falling on your head and clearing your entire body from head to toe, nourishing you with healing energy.

5   When you are able to feel the waterfall, change your breath to inhaling through your nose and then exhale with a dragon-breathing fire sound – don't be afraid to make as much noise as you need to.

6   Stay with this visualization and breathing technique until the timer bell rings.

7   Bring your breath back to a natural state, inhaling through your nose and exhaling through your nose. When you are ready, open your eyes.

Become the Most Productive Person You Know

Whenever we talk about creativity, we tend to forget to talk about how influenced it is by colour – the colours we work with, the colours we wear and the colours we surround ourselves with. Productivity, which is after all, energy, is strongly affected by colour energy.

Dark colours tend to be heavy on us; the energies don't move easily, but instead absorb and ask to stay within. They are great for contemplation and inward thought. I love wearing them when doing reflection exercises and deep meditation.

Whenever you feel you need to be more productive, however, you should avoid dark colours – especially around your chest, as energies here should always be free, open and responsive.

Colours that boost productivity are bright and light. They encourage us to move and bring more joy into a process. For example, I always wear yellow shoes to help me get a move on. If you're not comfortable wearing these colours, try placing magenta, yellow and cobalt blue on your desk to stimulate productivity.

Writing in Colour

Using different colours of pens to write will help keep your mind active and engaged. It is also a way to relax and improve creativity, as you are stimulating different emotions. Try these:

Magenta for innovative ideas.

Green for flow and growth.

Turquoise for writing from the heart.

Purple for writing stories and mysteries.

Manifesting Abundance

Try this manifestation meditation to bring more wealth,
both material and spiritual richness, into your life.

Green and gold are the classic colours of abundance, although you may wish to also work with the colours that most resonate for you in your daily spiritual practice. For example, I teach women in particular to use orange and magenta to manifest and create, as they are colours of intuition and energy. In the following exercise, we will explore two ways to work with colour to manifest abundance.

The colour green is associated with growth and nature, so in your work with this colour, be led by the planet Earth and the universe, and surrender your expectations to what is bigger than yourself. To start this journey, connect with your heart and forgive yourself.

One of the most powerful colour healers, the colour gold materializes any intention it is combined with, and it is used to help unseen things appear. You always need to remember that colours will help and lead you, but you must work on letting go of any beliefs, fears or actions that may keep you closed off from, or unreceptive to, the power of colour energy.

ABUNDANCE MEDITATION

You will need:

- Basil essential oil

- Oil burner

1   Light the candle in your oil burner and put three drops of the basil essential oil into the burner's water.

2   Sit on a straight-backed chair, facing the tealight in the burner, with your hands resting upwards on your lap, and allow your mind to become still while watching the flame. Ensure your feet are properly planted on the floor, evenly apart. Close your eyes.

3   Take three deep breaths, imagining as you do so that you are breathing in glittering green flames of light that drive out any areas of sludge-y, slow energy in your mind and body.

4   Once you feel fully cleansed by this vibrant green energy, begin to imagine a sparkling golden column of light shooting down from the heavens on to the top of your head and coursing through you to your feet.

5 Now imagine that the golden column of light is pooling in your tummy and emerges from your torso in a sphere. Hold the sphere of golden light in your hands and 'see' within it what your life will be like once you manifest the abundance you seek. For example, if you need money for a holiday, imagine yourself on that holiday. Really fill in the details; think about what you're wearing, what you're doing and how you feel. The more emotional energy you can put into this vision, the better.

6 When you have really connected with that image, send the sphere back up into the heavens, as if you're gently throwing a beach ball above your head.

7 Open your eyes, rub your hands together, stamp your feet a bit and, when ready, get up and move around.

Dress for Success

The colours we choose to wear, more often than not, tell our story before we speak. They inform the person we are interacting with about how we are feeling, what kind of person we are and so much more. Even if the person before you doesn't know anything about colour, their subconscious gets the message. Understanding the subliminal messages you send through the colours you choose to wear will help you create the first impression you desire.

When you want to present yourself as a team player.

Warm neutrals, such as beige paired with a small orange accessory. Warm neutrals will give the impression that you can accept different opinions and the orange accessory will show that you enjoy spending time with others.

When you want to show strong leadership.

Greys or whites paired with a touch of red. The grey will balance the strong energy of the red. White adds a sense of purity and honesty to red energy. Red is a colour of power, strength and shows strong leadership skills. Do you notice that male politicians wear a red tie when they want to communicate a strong message?

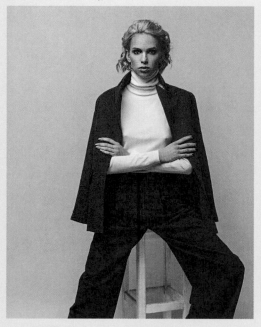

When you want to show that you are trustworthy and punctual.

Other than arriving on time, wearing dark blue (a light blue will give the message that you are relaxed) will give the impression that you are serious about work: you are trustworthy and reliable. This always works like a charm.

When you want to show that you are creative.

Blue trousers and a shirt with an orange, magenta and yellow combination. These colours together send the message that you are not afraid to express your ideas: you are willing to put yourself out there and create.

CHAPTER 5

Health & Wellbeing

'Try to be a rainbow
in someone's cloud.'

Maya Angelou

Working with colour taught me to prioritize my wellbeing and mental health. Using colour visualizations and related techniques are fast ways to help the nervous system relax and calm down, and this type of work also grounds and centres us mentally, emotionally and physically. It releases blocks and connects us to our inner world. Treating ourselves with compassion and kindness aids healing, and this chapter specifically includes exercises for self-care, health and wellbeing. With colour, the universe gave us the code to heal ourselves.

In the following pages, you will find stressbusters, aromatherapy remedies and breathing exercises for a quick fix when you are on the go. There is also a nutritional guide to help you understand why you are attracted to certain foods at different moments in your life and which colours of food can help common conditions such as low energy, poor digestion, detoxification and insomnia.

Stressbusters

Stress is something we all have to deal with on a daily basis; it keeps us on edge and drains our energies. When we are stressed, our bodies, minds and emotions don't function well. We are out of ideas, we can only see obstacles and we fail to come up with solutions that enhance our lives.

Anyone familiar with energy work knows that there are many aspects of modern society that can throw off our internal balance. In the age of Facebook and Instagram, you don't even need to be in the same room as someone to pick up on their energy – negative or positive. If you feel exhausted, cloudy-headed or emotionally disconnected, this surrounding negativity may be part of the problem.

At the end of the day, our energies are our own, and nobody else should be able to mess with them. Clearing your energy periodically will help keep the negative vibes away, and one of the best ways to do this is to use fragrance in combination with visualizations.

Herbal remedies and essential oils can evoke colour memories and imagery, and the fragrance can transport you to a more peaceful and calm state of mind. In addition, the fresh or dried leaves, flowers and roots of many plants can be safely ingested in teas, tinctures and food.

Lavender: Calms the nervous system and aids rest and sleep. Dab two drops of the oil on your wrists or use as a pillow spray.

Rose: Associated with rose pink energy, rose connects us to the energy of love and compassion, soothes emotions and balances hormones and mood. Add rose petals to tea or hot chocolate when you need to connect to love.

Chamomile: A soothing yellow energy, the chamomile flower helps calm the stomach, releases anxiety and promotes sleep. Drink the tea in a yellow mug to intensify its power.

Jasmine: The oil relieves stress, anxiety, depression and insomnia, and improves energy. Associated with the colour white, jasmine is good for cleansing the body and moving energy around. Use it as a room spray when you want to attract fresh starts and new beginnings.

Orange blossom: A soothing scent, this brings joy into a space. I love using it as a room spray before a gathering or when I'm feeling alone.

Clary sage: Good for your lungs and respiratory system, the oil has a soothing green energy. Drink a cup of sage herbal tea when you need to heal your heart from rejection or heartbreak.

ENERGY-CLEARING AURA BATH

You will need:

Relaxing music

Epsom salts

Rose quartz crystal (optional)

Amethyst crystal (optional)

Lavender or rose essential oil

Pink rose petals

Timer

Coloured lights
(alternatively, you can use
your imagination)

One way to recharge after a long day is with a colour aura bath that uses all the senses to balance you on a mind, body and soul level. Even if you don't have a bath, soaking your feet in a water bucket should do the trick!

1   Play your music and prepare the bath, keeping in mind your intention (see page 31) to cleanse your energy and raise your vibes with the warmth of the water.

2   Add 2 cups of Epsom salts and the rose quartz and amethyst, if using, while focusing on your intention. Then add a few drops of lavender or rose oil and drop in the rose petals.

3   Set your timer to 20 minutes with an alarm after every two minutes. Set your coloured lights to change every two minutes.

4   Get in the bath and take the first two minutes to relax.

5   Now envision all the colours of the rainbow, plus turquoise and gold, entering through the top of your head and moving to the tips of your toes with every breath. Imagine the colours clearing your entire energy.

LAVENDER BREATHING EXERCISE

Another quick exercise to release stress is to use lavender breathing. Lavender is a colour of calm, rest and gratitude. Lavender reminds us to be in love and have gratitude, and this meditation is an exercise in stillness, silence and peace. You want to create a space of neutrality, without extremes of happiness or negativity.

You will need:

- Lavender – either fresh stems, a candle or essential oil

- A quiet room for meditative breathing

1   Place a few drops of essential oil in a diffuser, or light your lavender candle. If you have fresh stems, crush them lightly to release their fragrance. The essential oil will be the most potent source.

2   This exercise can last from three to 10 minutes, depending on how much time you have. Set your timer for your chosen time.

3   Lay down flat on your back, restfully in your meditation space, with your spine straight and shoulders relaxed. Close your eyes.

4   Take five deep soft breaths through your nose, bringing your focus to the breath, the beauty of being alive and simply breathing. Let go of your thoughts, to-do lists and bring yourself to the moment.

5   Gently begin to breathe in the fragrance of lavender. Visualize yourself in a golden egg of energy floating in a field of lavender – experience the sights and smells while you bathe in the fragrant silence. Let the colour soothe and calm you.

6   When the timer goes off, take a deep inhale, release the breath and bring yourself back to the moment and the room. When you are ready, open your eyes.

Colours against Anxiety

Colours are excellent for reducing anxiety because they communicate directly with your nervous system and emotions. Have you ever walked into a room with intense colours and wanted to leave immediately, but walked into another and wanted to stay forever because it felt so good? It's the colours, I tell you!

I've put together some colour options for you to use when feeling anxious or sleepless. You can use these colours by wearing them, visualizing them, using them in meditation, or looking at them (but not from a screen if you are trying to sleep!).

Lavender: Acts as an instant calmer to the nervous system; it asks you to bring the connection of your body and mind into focus.

Lilac with a touch of pink and blue: Brings instant hope and asks you to find strength in your intuition and faith in order to soothe anxiety.

Peach: A warm hug, wrapped in sunshine, this colour is reminiscent of the playfulness of childhood, allowing you to be present and enjoy the moment without overthinking.

Pastel green: A neutralizing colour that helps you connect to your heart and find the depths of your strength and feeling.

Find Balance in Nutrition

Let's start by talking about the sun! The sun is our guide in our waking life; the sun gives us light and – via photosynthesis – the plants we eat convert this light into energy that benefits us physically.

As colour is our map to wellbeing, the colour of our food is also important: choosing colourful foods is a great way to help ourselves work through different emotions and understand our nutritional needs. Colour in plants indicates that phytochemicals – certain minerals and vitamins – are available. For example, carotenoids in red, orange, yellow, and green plants may inhibit cardiovascular disease and boost immunity; lutein in dark, leafy greens are linked to eye health.

Eating the colours of the rainbow as often as you can should be your goal. The more colours you have on your plate, the more nutrition you have in your belly. When food is grown in a chemical-free environment and absorbs the light it needs from the sun, it feeds different parts of your energy.

Red Foods

Red foods are wonderful for increasing energy, vitality and sexual appetite. They can give a much-needed energy boost when eaten at the end of a long week. Red foods contain powerful antioxidants, such as lycopene, a type of carotenoid connected to the health of certain lungs. Eat these especially when you are concerned about the heart, lungs and prostate.

Orange Foods

Great for healing inflammatory problems and stimulating the lower digestive system without overpowering it, orange foods are also good at breaking down fats and for harnessing emotional energy, and that feels satisfying in the belly. If you are going through a down time or feel depressed, use orange foods to elevate your mood.

Yellow Foods

These foods are uplifting, cleansing and are digestion aids and metabolism boosters. They are also great for eye and heart health because they contain lots of vitamin A. Yellow is also a mood and energy booster. If you are feeling depressed, but not anxious, have some pineapples or lemonade, which will help boost your energy on low days. Yellow foods are also useful when problem-solving and taking tests – their energy helps stimulate the mind.

Green Foods

Green foods help release anger from the body, helping to calm the orange and red energies in the body. Great alkalizers that help to flush toxins out of your body, green foods connect you with your divine heart. Practise mindful eating with green foods because they have a powerful vibration.

Blue and Purple Foods

These coloured foods aid sleep, promote dreams and strengthen visualization powers. They can help reduce anxiety and insomnia. Blue and purple fruits and vegetables have been shown to help slow the ageing process and improve memory. Research has found that eating blueberries helps with sleep troubles.

CHAPTER 6

Everyday Colour Hacks

*'Life is like a rainbow. You need both rain and sun
to make the colours appear.'*

Unknown

This chapter identifies ways in which you can use colour to get the most out of your day, every day. You do not need to incorporate each and every tip suggested here – try one and build up your practice over time.

The wonderful thing about colour is that it can be effective even when used in simple, small ways that don't require much effort. The mere presence of a colour can radically change your mood, whether it's the plate you use for your lunchtime sandwich or the red shoes you wear to go out for the evening.

These ideas will also help you come up with your own hacks, using colours in your home, work space and wardrobe that you know make you feel more confident, sleep deeper or imbue you with more positive energy.

A Shot of Confidence

You might have good days, and not so good days, when it comes to your confidence. Some days we believe we can conquer the world, other days we just can't. The first thing you need to do when you are struggling with your self-belief is to listen to your fears. Instead of trying to push away self-doubt, bring the doubt to you like a child and sit it in your lap, then ask yourself what it is that you need most now? What is your self-doubt trying to tell you? Listen to the first answer that comes to you.

CONFIDENCE BOOSTER

This exercise works like a little 'booster shot' of confidence, and it is not only good for the bad days but also for the good ones. Enjoy it whenever you need to build yourself up.

1   Set your timer for 10 to 15 minutes.

2   Sit in a lotus position, with your spine erect but relaxed. Close your eyes.

3   Take six deep breaths, letting all parts of your body release any tension you are holding on to.

4   In the centre of your body, wherever feels right for you, start building an image of a golden lotus flower. Start with visualizing it closed, and then open it with every inhale you take.

5   With every exhale, notice the lotus flower sending sparkles and glow to different parts of your body: your belly, chest, crown, face and legs.

6   Visualize yourself in a golden egg-shaped energy field.

7   Rest here until the timer bell rings, then take a deep inhale, exhale and bring yourself back to the moment and the room. When you are ready, open your eyes.

Sleep Deeper

Colour is the best sleep hacker!

If you have difficulty falling asleep
because of an active mind, make sure
you remove anything yellow from your
bed. White sheets won't be ideal either,
so choose warm neutrals such as beige
instead, as the colour is cosy without
being stimulating. We need to allow our bodies to be in a neutral
space for sleep to perform its healing duties during the night.

Blues, lavenders and lilacs are also instant relaxers. They encourage
more frequent dreaming, as they relax the mind but stimulate the
subconscious. However, if you have trouble waking up in the morning,
these colours won't help you, so either combine them with a neutral
or use neutrals alone. Peach-coloured bedding will help reduce
anxiety and make you feel positive.

SLEEP VISUALIZATION

This exercise will get you to sleep if you have trouble settling down, but it can also be used to help you return to sleep should you wake up in the middle of the night.

1   Set your timer for 20 minutes.

2   Lay in your bed, in a comfortable sleep position.

3   Close your eyes and take five deep breaths, inhaling for five and exhaling for five.

4   Gently close your right hand into a light fist, open it, then close the left one and open it.

5   Alternate the motion between your hands, while imagining the following colours entering your body from the top of your head to the tips of your toes, one by one. Slowly take five deep breaths with each colour.

1 Violet	**2** Navy blue	**3** Sky blue
4 Turquoise	**5** Rose pink	**6** Green
7 Warm yellow	**8** Peach	**9** Red

6   When the timer bell rings, take a deep inhale, then exhale and bring yourself back to the moment and the room. When you are ready, open your eyes.

Home Hacks

We spend at least 70 per cent of our lives indoors. Our homes reflect our inner world, which is why it is so important that our space supports us, makes us feel good and brings out the best in us. Colour is a powerful tool to bring energy, harmony, safety, creativity and much more into living spaces. It can easily be added with accessories, such as cushions, rugs, plant pots, faux flowers and linens, as well as bigger statement pieces, such as tables and sofas, or try painting just one wall a colour in an otherwise neutral setting.

Red Interiors

Red spaces are exciting and have a strong energizing impact. Add accents in the social areas of a home, especially in basements or in spaces that feel dull and depleted. If you want to encourage your appetite, add it to the dining room as well, but stay away from it in the kitchen if you want to diet! Add red to the bedroom to bring in more passion and intimacy, and use it in an office to send a message of power and leadership.

Orange Interiors

Socially inviting, orange encourages people to connect on an emotional level and to meet more frequently. Deeper orange shades are ideal for a dining room if you're a person who loves hosting and nurturing people with your food. Peach, a soft shade of orange, is a lovely colour for bedrooms, as it is soothing, nurturing and aids sleep.

Yellow Interiors

Such a positive colour, yellow brings sunshine and happiness into a space. Make sure you are using the deep shades of yellow when painting walls, however, as bright tones can create anxiety for sensitive people. This is a colour that reminds people to be energized, joyful and excited – I wouldn't use it in the bedroom because it's such a stimulating colour. In small doses, yellow is ideal in an office or study space to increase productivity.

Teal Interiors

Ideal for couples who have just moved in together, teal is a colour that helps people communicate better and feel safe. An open and vulnerable colour, it is comfortable without being dull. It is particularly suitable for a family that has difficulty talking and opening up. It's an ideal colour for most rooms in the home.

Brown Interiors

A grounding colour, brown symbolizes tradition and family, but too much can make us feel stuck. Brown is never the right choice for bedrooms: it makes people feel stagnant and unable to move – trust me I've tried it! Brown is useful for entrances and outdoor spaces that require a connection with the earth.

Clothing Colour Hacks

One of the most important ways colours affect us is with the clothes we put on. When we wear colour, we are telling the world *'Hey this is how I feel today'* or even *'This is who I am'*. As light falls on our clothes, it reflects or absorbs the colour, affecting the colour vibration of what we are wearing. This doesn't mean that you have to be a walking rainbow; you can bring colour into your closet in a way that is stylish, simple and trendy.

If you tend to stay away from bold colours – or from colour altogether – and wear mostly black or neutrals, consider starting with accessories, such as a handbag, shoes or a scarf, in a colour first. Here

are some of my tips on using colour in clothing to enhance your mood or put you in a positive frame of mind.

Black

A controversial colour, many spiritual teachers ask you to stay away from black. Some psychologists even say that to wear it is a sign of depression. For many, however, black is easy, simple and straightforward: they live

in black and they feel fine. Black is one of the colours I have in my closet, but I use it with caution. It is a colour that protects us, hides our imperfections and many cultures use it as a mourning colour. But black clothing can become an issue if you are unable to wear anything else. You might want to ask yourself if you feel like you need to blend in, and why that might be? Think about the colours that bother you the most and explore what they mean to you. Would you never wear red? Could it be that you need to let go of past painful experiences and find some courage in the area of love and passion?

Black is often a go-to colour when you're having a bad day, but be aware of this, as black absorbs all energy around you and can make you feel extra sensitive. If you are having a bad day, but can't face wearing anything too bright, wear white instead.

On the other hand, black is an ideal choice if you want to feel grounded. I love wearing it on my feet when I'm having a crazy day, running around all over the place. I never wear it to sleep in because it doesn't allow energy to move around the body. For sleep, wear light neutrals instead.

White

We see white because it reflects all the colours. As it is not an absorbing colour, you can use white on sensitive days to feel fresh and rejuvenated. White is the colour of new beginnings, purity and permission; it can also give you feelings of flowing and openness. Mixing white with another colour helps to reflect the bright side of that colour. For example, if you wear white with magenta, you are reflecting creativity and innovation. This combination is one of my all-time favourites.

Red

Red puts you in the centre of attention – if you are an extrovert, you will thrive when wearing it. Red is a great energy booster, so wear it to the gym if you want to keep your energy up and train harder. If you are unable to wake up in the morning, try scheduling coloured lights to shine red with your alarm. You will thank me later.

Orange

Orange connects us with the joy within. You can work with orange in your wardrobe by pairing an orange accessory or scarf with clothes on days when you feel lonely and in need of a lift.

Rose Pink

This is my favourite colour to work with, because rose pink is the colour of kindness, compassion and purity in love. I believe that we

need these energies a lot these days. Whenever I am working on something that requires me to leave my comfort zone, I put on something pink to remind me to be compassionate with myself. You can use this colour in a scarf or a shirt, too. During difficult days, I wear pink to soften my energy.

Turquoise

Wear this colour when you want to communicate from the heart: when you want to get in touch with your desires, but also feel protected. Wearing this colour helps you channel ancient wisdom, openness and empathy. This is a soothing colour for empaths.

Green

Green is a wonderful colour to stimulate growth and organic movement, especially when you are working on increasing money or abundance. Unfortunately, green clothing does not sell well – a study showed that magazine covers featuring models wearing green sold the least, so if you are going out on a date, save that green dress for a meeting with friends instead.

Cyan Blue

This shade of blue is a confidence booster; it sends a message that you are trustworthy, confident and vibrant. Wear this colour when you are looking to show yourself as a positive communicator, approachable and reliable.

Magenta

This colour acts as a magnet. Whenever you wear it, make sure you are focusing on the things that you want in your life, because this colour will bring them to you. I use this colour when I want to work on manifestation, and when I'm feeling really positive, to bring in more of the things I want. It's a great colour to wear as a shirt, bracelet, scarf or even as a headband if you want to generate new ideas for a project.

Colour Cleanse Your Home

Your home has energies that are important for your wellbeing. Cleansing your home – by using visualization techniques and smudging (burning herbs and replacing negative energy with new fresh positive energy) – will help shift that energy and dispel negative vibrations. Just like the body, the home can pick up negative and static energies and past emotions. These are usually heavy and love to stay in corners. You know that your home has low vibration energies when you feel heavy and unable to relax at home. It is important to cleanse these energies regularly so you can thrive, welcome in new energies and get rid of what no longer serves you.

A home can pick up energies from various sources: electronics can create heavy energy; arguments store negativity; old items that we never use and clutter create stagnant energy. It is especially important to clear the home after a romantic break-up, losing or leaving a job, or any major negative life event.

Releasing stuck energy can result in things moving out of your home and life, and more positive feelings coming in. Sleeping will be easier and deeper. Conversations will flow naturally with fewer arguments. You will feel more centred and be able to stay in the moment consistently. Cleansing your home is a great message to the universe that you are ready to welcome abundance and love into your life. Negative energy takes space, so letting it go makes way for new things to enter.

Herbal Cleansing

One of the most popular techniques for clearing energy in the home is to burn herbs. They increases the oxygen supply to the brain, clear away germs from the air and the smell aids relaxation. Here are some of the herbs to use.

White sage smudge sticks: clears away negative energy and brings an energy of transformation.

Lavender: for balance, peace and relaxation.

Cedar: purifies, heals and attracts positive energy.

Rosemary: a powerful healer that brings clarity to challenges (and it also attracts love).

HOME ENERGY CLEARING

You will need:

- White sage or any clearing herb stick (pick one from the list on page 195, or create your own by bundling the herbs and tying tightly with twine)

- A large, clear glass of water

- A white candle and a candle in another colour that represents your desire. For example, choose a green candle for abundance; red to attract love and passion; pink to attract gratitude and unconditional love

1   Take a few minutes to look around your space. What items haven't you used in the last six months? Donate them or give them to someone who would love them. Then clear any clutter, and put items in their place.

2   Open the windows, setting the intention to let the energies that don't belong there to leave through the windows.

3   Close your eyes, set an intention of letting go of what no longer serves your highest good. Light your stick.

4   Walk around your home slowly, focusing on your intention of letting go of what no longer serves your highest good.

5   I usually like to recite this incantation: *'Whatever doesn't belong here leave, whatever is not for the highest good for everyone here, leave.'*

6   Make sure you take your time around corners, electronics and bathrooms. Enjoy the process and feel it in your heart when you've finished with each room.

7   Extinguish the herbal stick and close the windows. Pick up the glass of water (you can add salt to it) and walk around the house, holding it with the strong intention to purify and cleanse the home; the water will collect lower-frequency energies.

8   Pour the water down the toilet and flush (this is a symbol that you want these low energies out of your home).

9   Now sit in the centre of your home or in your meditation space and visualize the earth's core pumping red light into your home, from floor to ceiling and to all four corners of your home. Visualize the colour changing to orange, then yellow, then green, sky blue, indigo and finally violet.

10   Let the violet colour turn into a violet flame and visualize it burning away all the energies that no longer serve you. Seal your home with a golden light in all corners.

11   Visualize pulling golden cords from the four corners of your home to meet together in the centre, then visualize grounding them to the centre of the earth (see also the grounding exercise, on page 35).

12   Take a few deep breaths, focus on the positive energy you want to attract to your home. Light your two candles and let their flames spread your beautiful intentions throughout your home.

Nourish Your Energy

On busy days, weeks or months, your energy can feel depleted and you can easily forget that you have infinite energy inside of you that can be harnessed to nourish yourself, at any time you need it. I tend to have busy days filled with interactions with people, and this next exercise always brings me back to my reservoir of energy, refuels me and helps me find that peace I seek to continue working.

ENERGY-HARNESSING EXERCISE

Whenever you feel depleted or down, use this visualization to help zap you back into action and creativity.

1   Set your timer for 15 to 20 minutes.

2   Bring your right hand to the top of your head and gently touch your crown.

3   Gently place your left hand on your diaphragm. Close your eyes.

4   Breathing softly, inhale for four counts and exhale for five counts. Keep repeating.

5   Now start visualizing a loop of energy coursing from your root chakra to your crown chakra (see page 37).

6   Visualize all the colours of the chakras, one by one, coursing through this loop of energy.

7   In your own time, once you have visualized all the colours, imagine the energy loop resting in your sacral chakra, steady, balanced and always there when you need it.

8   Finally visualize a beam of gold surrounding your entire body, keeping your energy and balance sealed in and protected.

9   When the timer rings, take a deep breath and open your eyes.

Conclusion

I hope this book has shown you how colour can contribute to transforming your life. Colour is one of the doors that, when you walk through it, show you the beautiful language of your intuition and inner voice. It will help you turn your challenges into your greatest assets. It is powerful beyond measure.

Remember, life is not linear: it moves organically with setbacks, wins, turns, twists and constant change. Every time you expect linear achievements from yourself, call yourself out because it is not true. Learn to respect the so-called negative emotions, learn to hear their voice and have emotional flexibility. The bad days are as important as the beautiful ones.

No matter what your background or social conditioning has been, or your past struggles with patience, compassion and reflection, you have the power to turn it all around.

One of the most important things I want you to take from this book is that colour is always communicating with us, because the universe is. Remember to listen to that voice when it nudges you. Listen and allow yourself to be guided, even if it doesn't seem to be the plan you had in mind. Trust that the universe with all its shades and shadows is always looking out for you. Usually with a grander plan for you.

The way my life is right now is not because I controlled it, but because I gave the lead to the universe within me. I look around and I know that the universe heard me; it heard my cries, my needs and my desires.

With every twist and turn, learn to trust your inner voice and have faith in yourself above all.

I love you!

Walaa xx

INDEX

N
numerology 72–3
nutrition 177–9

O
orange 33, 41–3, 77, 142
 clothing 191
 exercises using 109,
  112–13, 144–5
 foods 179
 home interiors 186
 month 93, 96
 personality 76

P
pastel colours 65–9, 175
peach 41, 175, 186
 exercises using 135
pens, coloured 137, 157
perception of colour 11
pink 33, 66
 exercises using 121,
  123–4, 140–1
 see also rose pink
Pleasonton, Augustus 21
productivity 156
purple 157
 foods 179
 see also lavender
  and lilac

Q
questions 16–17, 103,
 109, 114, 120, 122, 126,
 146, 148

R
red 38–40, 74, 105
 clothing 189, 190
 foods 177
 home interiors 186
 month 93, 96
 personality 75
rose pink 29, 66, 105,
 140, 169, 191

S
sacral chakra 42–3
self-care list 26
self-development 71,
 92–6
self-forgiveness 50, 121,
 131, 148, 159
self-love 66, 99, 101
 blockages 104–8
 healing 109–42
self-talking 102
sexuality 41, 42
shadow side 29, 68
sleep 184–5, 189
solar plexus chakra 45–6
stressbusters 168–73
subconscious 11, 28, 37,
 101, 131, 164, 184
sunlight 18–19, 21, 44,
 79, 177

T
teal 187
third eye chakra 58–60
throat chakra 53–5
timing of exercises 27

tints 65
truth 52, 53, 54
turquoise 157, 192

U
unconditional love 49,
 66, 80, 108, 121, 148,
 196

V
violet 33, 61–4, 86
 exercises using 115–17
 month 95
 personality 87
visualizing colours 30

W
water 27, 42, 145, 155,
 171, 196
wavelengths 38, 41, 44,
 52, 61
white 33, 65, 189, 190
wisdom 56, 58, 61
work and career 150–65
writing in colour 157

Y
yellow 17, 32, 44–6, 78
 exercises using 109,
  111, 115, 118–20
 foods 179
 home interiors 187
 month 93, 96
 pale yellow 68
 personality 79

Author Acknowledgements

Thank you Stacey Jessop and Oliver Coulter for believing in me, this project, the late nights we all put in to bring this book to life. Thank you Lisa Dyer and Jo Lal for seeing the potential in this book before I did and for making this dream a reality. Thank you David Perrota, for being my first guide and bringing me out of my shell.

Picture Credits

Courtesy © Walaa Al-Muhaiteeb: 172, 178, 191t, 203 ; 6, 13, 97 /Ruta Kenstaviciute;10, 14 /Gemma Rozas; 126, 131, 149, 188, 193 /Julia Malinowska **Pexels.com:** 156 Pixaby **Shutterstock Inc.:** 4tl Boule; 4tc Sunny Forest; 4cl Thanu Garapakdee; 4cc Poznyakov; 4bl Jonathan Martindale; 4br Neale Cousland; 8–9 Hybrid_Graphics; 18 Stig Alenas; 19 leoks; 20l Amnartk; 20r, 24–5, 186t Africa Studio; 21, 23, 28, 70–1, 98–9, 100, 102–3, 107, 150–1, 166–7, 201 Benjavisa Ruangvaree Art; 31 Netrun78; 33, 59, 63, 116 dityazemli; 36 Reamolko; 38, 42, 45, 50, 53, 58, 62 Suto Norbert Zsolt; 49 Abo Photography; 54 Kite_rin; 60 Elenarts; 64 Klavdiya Krinichnaya; 66 Pushish Images; 67 Feel good studio; 68 Maridav; 69 panattar; 81 imnoom; 86 Odem1970; 90 Kumar Jatinder; 93t Marie C Fields; 93c Irina Burakova; 93b FamVeld; 94t Romolo Tavani; 94c Panu Ruangjan; 94b visionteller; 95t Garry0305; 95c Printemps PhotoArt; 95b Piti Tan; 96t catmanc; 96c An Nguyen; 96b Subbotina Anna; 104 Zodar; 110 ra2 studio; 112 Jag_cz; 113 YamabikaY; 114 Sneha Cecil; 117 Sirikan Aka; 118 Christian Sterk; 120 Feaspb; 122 atiger; 124 TierneyMJ; 129 tomertu; 133 o0hyperblaster; 134 rania bdn; 136 Azurhino; 137 Barbara Neveu; 140 Undrey; 141, 197 Microgen; 143 Natalia Romanova; 147 S.Gvozd; 152 Wirestock Creators; 162 Madeleine Steinbach; 164 Cozy Home; 165t Shadska Photo; 165b Victoria Chudinova; 169 Sensay; 170 9dream studio; 174 almaje; 176 Denise I Johnson; 182 HappyLizard; 184 stockfour; 186b Interior Design; 187 Mallmo; 189 Nick Starichenk; 190 Aila Images; 191b Maria Markevich; 192 Andrei Park; 195 JurateBuiviene; 196 Shelli Jensen **Twenty Twenty:** 4tr Dan Dedekind, 4cr Terri Sitrin, 4bc Bree Johnson, 82 Linda@ lindaze; 85 @pablorobledo_co;160 Bowonpat Sakaew **Unsplash:** 34 Juan Manuel Núñez Méndez; 47 James Day; 57 Chirag Nayak; 128 Artem Kniaz; 139 David Brooke Martin; 154–5 Adrien Olichon; 163 Prajwal Vedpathak; 199 Pawel Czerwinski **Thanks to Stacey Jessop:** 26–7, 30, 32, 33c, 154, 157, 161, 171

About Us

Welbeck Balance is dedicated to changing lives. Our mission is to deliver life-enhancing books to help improve your wellbeing so that you can live with greater clarity and meaning, wherever you are on life's journey.

Welbeck Balance is part of the Welbeck Publishing Group – a globally recognized, independent publisher based in London. Welbeck are renowned for our innovative ideas, production values and developing long-lasting content. Our books have been translated into over 30 languages in more than 60 countries around the world.

If you love books, then join the club and sign up to our newsletter for exclusive offers, extracts, author interviews and more information.

To find out more and sign up visit: www.welbeckpublishing.com.

twitter.com/welbeckpublish

Instagram.com/welbeckpublish

Facebook.com/welbeckuk